Everyday Chemistry

Published by
Heron Books, Inc.
20950 SW Rock Creek Road
Sheridan, OR 97378

heronbooks.com

Special thanks to all the teachers and students who
provided feedback instrumental to this edition.

Second Edition © 2004, 2024 Heron Books
All Rights Reserved

ISBN: 978-0-89-739015-6

Any unauthorized copying, translation, duplication or distribution, in whole or in part, by any means, including electronic copying, storage or transmission, is a violation of applicable laws.

The Heron Books name and the heron bird symbol are registered trademarks of Delphi Schools, Inc.

Printed in the USA

29 February 2024

Everyday Chemistry

At Heron Books, we think learning should be engaging and fun. It should be hands-on and allow students to move at their own pace.

To facilitate this we have created a learning guide that will help any student progress through this book, chapter by chapter, with confidence and interest.

Get learning guides at
heronbooks.com/learningguides.

For teacher resources,
such as a final exam, email
teacherresources@heronbooks.com.

We would love to hear from you!
Email us at *feedback@heronbooks.com.*

CONTENTS

Chapter 1
CHEMISTRY IS ALL AROUND US 1
    Chemistry at Home 1
    Making Chemistry Work for Us 2

Chapter 2
GETTING STARTED WITH CHEMISTRY 3
    Matter and Atoms 3
    Molecules 4
    Chemicals and Chemistry 5

Chapter 3
SPACE BETWEEN MOLECULES 7
    Solids, Liquids and Gases 7
    Spaces Between Molecules 8
        Activity 1 Reduce Some Space between Molecules 9

Chapter 4
ELEMENTS AND ATOMS 11

Chapter 5
MOLECULES AND COMPOUNDS 13
        Mixtures and Pure Substances 16

Chapter 6
CHEMICAL REACTIONS 17
        Activity 2 Carbon Dioxide Cannon 19

Chapter 7
PROCEDURES 21
    Basic Safety 21

    Two Simple Procedures 22

    Activity 3 Procedures Practice 24

    Activity 4 Grow Crystals of Sugar: Start 25

Chapter 8
CARBON AND CANDLE CHEMISTRY 27

    Activity 5 Candle Chemistry #1 29

    Activity 6 Candle Chemistry #2 30

    Activity 7 Candle Chemistry #3 31

Chapter 9
WRITING CHEMICAL REACTIONS 33

Chapter 10
SUGAR AND CARBON 37

    Activity 8 Burn a Sugar Cube 39

Chapter 11
OXYGEN AND ITS REACTIONS 41

    Activity 9 Use Up Oxygen with Fire 43

    Activity 10 Make Writing Disappear 45

Chapter 12
OXIDIZING IRON 47

    Activity 11 Produce Rust 48

    Activity 12 Burn Iron 50

Chapter 13
MORE ABOUT WRITING CHEMICAL REACTIONS 53

Chapter 14
USING HYDROGEN PEROXIDE TO PRODUCE OXYGEN 57
- Catalysts 57
- Activity 13 Elephant's Toothpaste 59
  - More Hydrogen Peroxide Activities 61

Chapter 15
CARBON DIOXIDE 63
- Carbon Dioxide in the Air 63
- Carbon Dioxide in Rocks 63
- Activity 14 Release Carbon Dioxide from Antacid Tablets 65

Chapter 16
PUTTING CARBON DIOXIDE TO WORK 67
- Carbon Dioxide Gas Expands 67
- Carbon Dioxide Chokes Out Fire 67
- Activity 15 Carbon Dioxide Cannon (Repeat) 69
- Activity 16 Carbon Dioxide Fire Extinguisher #1 71
- Activity 17 Carbon Dioxide Fire Extinguisher #2 73

Chapter 17
ACIDS AND BASES 75
- Activity 18 Taste a Safe Acid and a Safe Base 76

Chapter 18
A QUICK LOOK AT ELECTRICITY 77
- Electricity 77

Chapter 19
ELECTRICITY AND ATOMS 79

Chapter 20
CHARGED ATOMS 83
- Ions 83

Chapter 21
WHAT MAKES ACIDS AND BASES OPPOSITE? 85
    Acids Have Positive H^+ Ions 86
    Bases Have Negative OH^- Ions 87

Chapter 22
THE REACTION WHEN ACID MEETS BASE 89
    The First Half of the Reaction 89
    The Second Half of the Reaction 90
    Both Halves of the Reaction Together 91
    A Dramatic Example of a Neutralization Reaction 92
    Activity 19 Neutralization Reaction 94

Chapter 23
A SCALE OF THE STRENGTHS OF ACIDS AND BASES 97
    Showing Acids and Bases with a Color Change 99
    Activity 20 Make a Red Cabbage Indicator 100
    Activity 21 Using an Acid-Base Indicator 102
    Activity 22 Test for Acids and Bases with Cabbage Juice
        Indicator 104
    Activity 23A Ammonia Cleaner, Epsom Salt and Vinegar 107
    Activity 23B Washing Soda, Epsom Salt and Lemon Juice 110

Chapter 24
CRYSTALS 113
    Growing Crystals 114
    Some Crystals Hold Water 114
    Colorful Crystals of Copper 114
    Activity 24 Grow Crystals of Sugar: Finish 116
    Activity 25 Grow Salt Crystals 118
    Activity 26 Grow Epsom Salt Crystals on Glass 120
    Activity 27 Get Water Out of Crystals 121
    Activity 28 Copper Penny Colors 123

Chapter 25
HOW SOAPS WORK 125
- Soap Chemistry 125
- Activity 29 How Soap Works 128

Chapter 26
"HARD" WATER 131
- Making Hard Water "Softer" 133
- Activity 30 Make Water Softer 135

Chapter 27
OXYGEN AND CARBON DIOXIDE 137
- Changing Sugar into Alcohol and Carbon Dioxide 138
- Activity 31 Make Alcohol and Carbon Dioxide with Yeast 140

Chapter 28
OXYGEN FROM PLANTS 143
- Activity 32 Oxygen from Plant Leaves 147

Chapter 29
ELECTRICITY IN CHEMISTRY 151
- Electricity Can Break Apart Water Molecules 151
- Energy 152
- Activity 33 Split Water Molecules with Electricity 153
- Activity 34 Use Electricity to Collect Hydrogen Gas 155

Chapter 30
CHEMICALS AND LIGHT 161
- Activity 35 Glow Water 162
- Activity 36 Glowing Highlighters 163
- Activity 37 Find Other Things that Glow 164

Chapter 31
MILK CHEMISTRY 165
- Plastic from Milk 165

Using Milk to Show Molecular Motion 165

Activity 38 Make Plastic from Milk 167

Activity 39 Make a Milk Rainbow 169

Chapter 32
METAL CHEMISTRY 171

Activity 40 Make "Silver" and Golden Pennies 172

Chapter 33
SLIME 177

Activity 41 Make Slime (Also Called Gak) 179

Activity 42 Make Bouncy Slime 181

Chapter 34
COLORED FLAMES FROM METAL COMPOUNDS 183

Activity 43 Flame Tests—Colored Flames from Metals 184

Activity 44 Flame Test Unknown Chemicals 186

Chapter 35
A GLANCE FORWARD 187

APPENDIX 189

More about Electrical Charge 191

History 191

Summary 192

Glossary 195

Materials Needed for the Activities in this Book 203

Chapter 1

Chemistry Is All Around Us

Everything around us is made of chemicals, including our bodies.

When you breathe, eat, or just sit and read, chemistry is involved. Your body is mostly made up of a chemical—water!

What we eat consists of thousands of chemicals which interact to give us what we need for energy and growth. Vitamins, minerals and medicines are all just particular chemicals or combinations of chemicals.

Chemistry is the scientific study of chemicals, what they are made of, their structure, and how they change when they combine or interact with other chemicals.

We will learn exactly what *chemicals* are in the next chapter, but first let's take a look at some of the ways knowledge of chemistry can be put to use.

CHEMISTRY AT HOME

Chemistry shows us how food changes as we cook it, how our bodies use the food we eat, how to preserve food, and even how food spoils.

Chemistry explains how cleaners work. We use chemistry to help decide what cleaner is best for dishes, laundry, our bodies and our homes. If we didn't have chemicals to use in cleaning up, we could get very sick. So we are using chemistry when we use bleaches and disinfectants, and even ordinary soap and water.

CHEMISTRY IS ALL AROUND US

Every action that changes a substance or uses one substance to change another substance involves chemicals interacting with each other. Burning things, using soap to clean up grease, fertilizing plants—all these kinds of activities involve chemicals interacting, and are understood and controlled by a knowledge of chemistry.

MAKING CHEMISTRY WORK FOR US

Some things in life are made just by controlling the shape of a substance, like cutting wood to make lumber or bending metal for pipes. Mostly that sort of thing does not involve much chemistry.

But an enormous number of the things that are built or manufactured require an understanding and use of chemistry. Businesses that make things like plastics, paints and some kinds of metal material use chemistry to make their products.

We use chemistry to make the fuels we burn in our cars, trucks, airplanes and space vehicles. And, of course, when we burn those fuels, that is chemistry at work again. Chemistry is used in electronics and communications industries to make computer chips, other parts of computers and electronic devices.

Some of the electrical power we use is created by chemical activity. The energy stored in batteries is released by chemical changes inside the batteries.

Chemistry is all around us all the time. Sometimes it is very helpful to know something about what is going on. Learning about chemistry will help you understand how the physical world works.

In this book, you'll find out many of the basics of chemistry. You'll get to use what you learned by doing many different activities that show how we create and control things through chemistry.

And you'll have some fun!

Chapter 2

Getting Started with Chemistry

To understand what chemistry is and how it works, it's helpful to start with atoms and molecules.

MATTER AND ATOMS

Matter is anything that has weight and takes up space. It can be solid (like wood), liquid (like water), or a gas (like air).

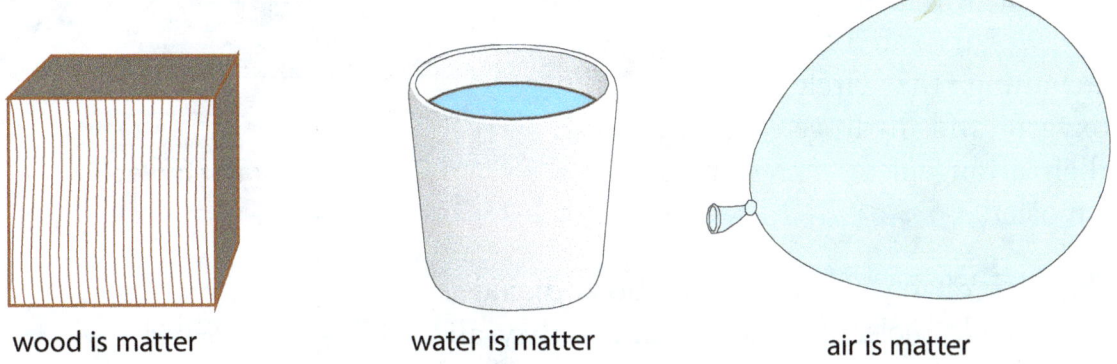

wood is matter   water is matter   air is matter

all matter takes up space

All matter is made up of tiny bits called **atoms**. Atoms are so very small that it takes an enormous number of them even to be visible. For example, a drop of water has 5,000,000,000,000,000,000,000 atoms in it! (In words, that is five sextillion atoms.) Atoms are *really* small.

Atoms combine in many ways to make up all the substances we encounter, like wood, water, air, bone, etc. All these substances are what we call matter.

GETTING STARTED WITH CHEMISTRY

There are about 100 different kinds of atoms in nature. Some examples you have probably heard of are hydrogen, oxygen and carbon. You will meet several more as we go along.

MOLECULES

Some atoms can "connect up" or stick together in groups called **molecules**. A molecule has at least two atoms in it.

With 100 kinds of atoms to start with, and so many ways they can connect together to make molecules, you can imagine that there are enormous numbers of different kinds of molecules.

We say that two molecules are of the same kind (or are "alike") if they both contain the same kind and number of atoms, arranged in the same way in the group.

Water is an example of a substance that is made up of one kind of molecule. Water molecules are all alike—they all have one oxygen atom and two hydrogen atoms, and they are always arranged in the same way. This can be illustrated by imagining the circles shown are oxygen and hydrogen atoms, and their arrangement represents a water molecule.

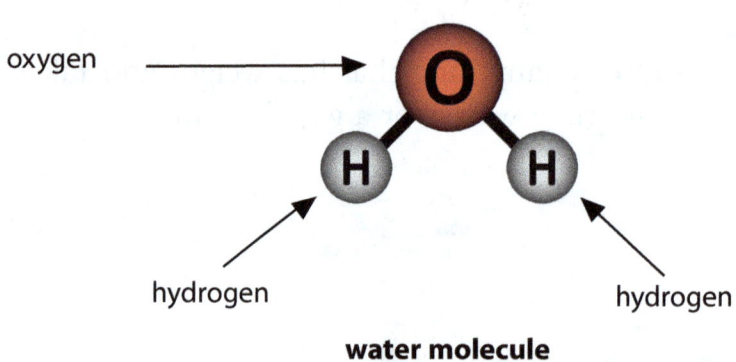
water molecule

You have probably heard of carbon dioxide. Carbon dioxide molecules are all alike—they all have one carbon atom and two oxygen atoms, always arranged the same way.

Molecules come in all different sizes. Water molecules have just three atoms in them, but sugar molecules have 45 atoms. Some molecules even contain hundreds of atoms!

Different molecules behave very differently. Water molecules form a liquid, carbon dioxide molecules form a gas, and sugar molecules form a solid.

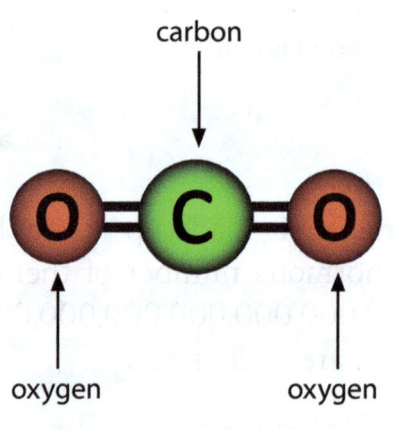
carbon dioxide molecule

GETTING STARTED WITH CHEMISTRY

CHEMICALS AND CHEMISTRY

And now it's time to learn exactly what a chemical is!

Let's start with what a chemical is *not*. Some substances contain various kinds of molecules. Wood is an example of a substance with many kinds of molecules, and air is an example with several kinds.

We call the kind of substance that has various kinds of molecules a **mixture**. We have lots of mixtures in our environment—dirt is a mixture, food is a mixture, etc.

In chemistry, we are mostly interested in the kind of substance that has just one kind of (atom or) molecule.

A **chemical** is a pure substance that is made up of only one kind of molecule or atom. Water, carbon dioxide and sugar are examples of chemicals. They are pure because all their molecules are the same. Gold, iron and aluminum are also examples of chemicals. In their cases, they are pure because all their *atoms* are the same. Their atoms don't link up to make molecules.

So, again, **chemistry** is the scientific study of chemicals, what they are made of, their structure, and how they change when they combine or interact with other chemicals.

Chapter 3

Space Between Molecules

SOLIDS, LIQUIDS AND GASES

Remember that matter is anything that has weight and takes up space. Of course, matter is made up of atoms and molecules. Any particular chunk of matter may be just one kind of atom or molecule, which we call a chemical. Or it could be some sort of mixture of different kinds of atoms and molecules.

The word **material** can be used to indicate some particular kind of matter. It's not a very exact meaning, just a way to speak of particular pieces or sorts of matter.

There are different ways to classify matter. One way is by whether a material has a definite shape or not. For instance, solids have a definite shape, but liquids and gases do not. Liquids flow and take the shape of a container. Gases expand to fill whatever space is available.

solid
(holds its shape)

liquid
(takes shape of container)

gas
(can expand if there is room)

SPACES BETWEEN MOLECULES

There are spaces between molecules in all substances. Generally, the molecules in a liquid are much closer together than molecules in a gas. This is because gases in the air expand to fill all the space they can, so the molecules can be very spread out. In a solid, the molecules are usually even closer together.

Solid　　　　　　　　Liquid　　　　　　　　Gas

ACTIVITY 1
Reduce Some Space between Molecules

For this activity, you will need:
- test tubes, 20 mL or larger (2 identical)
- tap water
- food coloring (two colors)
- isopropyl alcohol (approx. 90%)
- marker (thin) or masking tape

Information:

We have learned that there are spaces between molecules. In this activity, we will look at an example with liquids.

If you add ¼ cup water and ¼ cup alcohol, you should get ½ cup total, right?

But no, you don't.

This activity shows there are empty spaces in the liquids and that the total volume actually is less because some of the spaces get partially filled up.

Procedure:

1. Make a horizontal mark on one test tube a little below halfway up.

2. Very carefully, fill the test tube with water exactly to your mark. This is amount A and we will call this test tube A. Pour it into the test tube B.

3. Repeat step 2 so that test tube B has exactly 2 times amount A in it. Carefully make a mark on test tube B at the top of the water.

4. Empty and dry both test tubes.

5. Add a drop of one color to tube A and carefully fill it with water exactly to its mark. Pour into tube B.

SPACE BETWEEN MOLECULES

6. Rinse and dry tube A, add a drop of the other color to it and carefully fill it with alcohol exactly to its mark.

7. Very gently pour the alcohol into tube B, minimizing mixing. The alcohol will mostly float above the water, as the colors should show.

   Because the two liquids haven't mixed much, the volume may be nearly up to the mark in tube B, as you might expect.

8. Plug the tube with a stopper or your thumb and lightly mix by turning it upside down several times until the color is fairly uniform. Carefully observe the level of the liquid compared to your mark.

Results:

The volume should be slightly less than the mark made on step 2, even though you have put a full A amount of liquid into the tube twice.

We are seeing that some water molecules are fitting in among the alcohol molecules and vice versa, filling in some of the spaces between the molecules, reducing the amount of empty space. So, the volume is less!

Chapter 4
Elements and Atoms

Instead of saying "kind of atom" or "type of atom" all the time, chemists use the word **element**. Each kind of atom is an element—hydrogen is an element, carbon is an element. Gold and iron are elements. Some other familiar elements are aluminum, oxygen, helium, copper and chlorine. In nature, there are about 100 different elements.

When you speak, for instance, of "the element oxygen" you can mean a single atom of oxygen, an oxygen molecule of two oxygens, or a whole tankful of oxygen—it's all the element oxygen.

In some elements, like iron or carbon, the atoms are not connected to each other to make molecules. In others, like both hydrogen and oxygen, the atoms pair up into simple molecules (two hydrogens in a hydrogen molecule and two oxygens in an oxygen molecule).

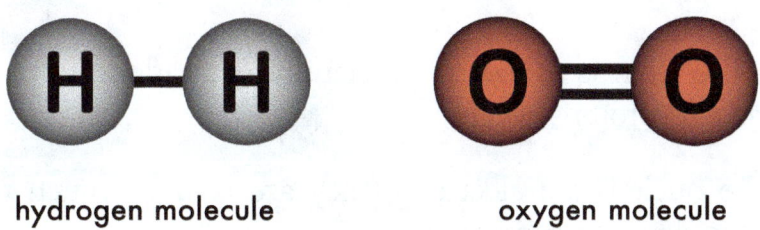

hydrogen molecule   oxygen molecule

Scientists are naturally very interested in getting a better understanding of the structure inside an atom.

Atoms are so small that only special kinds of microscopes called electron microscopes can get any kind of image of them. But even with these microscopes, the images are not very clear and don't show much of the inside of atoms. So the search for the structure of atoms has not been easy.

ELEMENTS AND ATOMS

Scientists have invented various models to try to illustrate the structure of atoms. While none of them is perfect, they can help us understand why atoms behave the way they do. Here is an example:

ATOM STRUCTURE

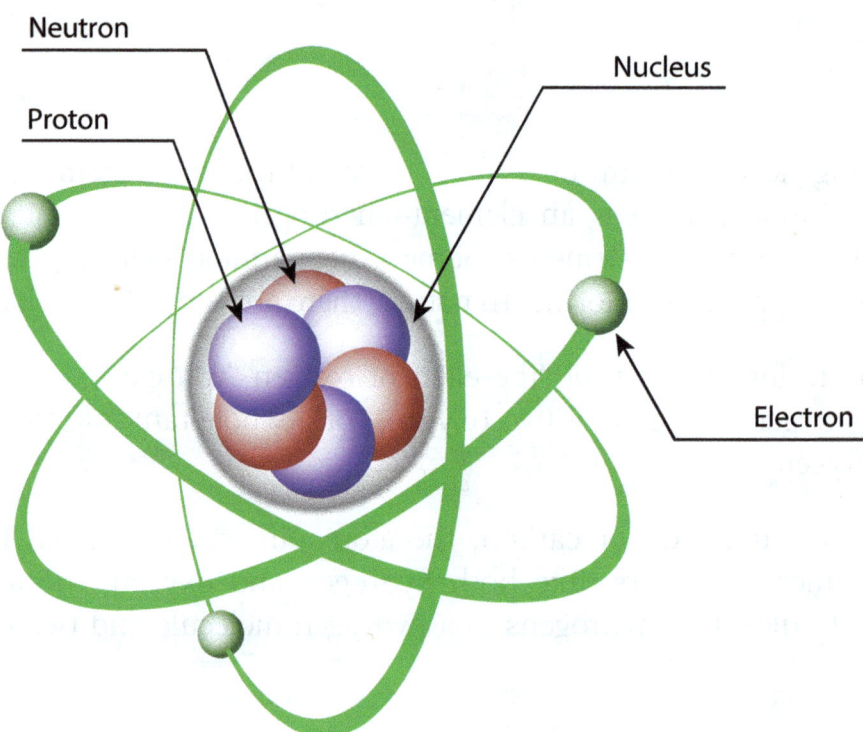

The center part of the atom is called the nucleus. It is made up of two kinds of tiny bits called neutrons and protons.

Orbiting around the nucleus are electrons (they are actually much tinier and much farther away than the drawing can show).

Chapter 5

Molecules and Compounds

As we have learned, a molecule is a tiny unit of matter made up of two or more atoms connected to one another.

The way atoms are grouped and arranged determines the different chemicals.

Here you can see some illustrations of molecules that show the number of atoms and how they are arranged. Both things are important. Advanced chemistry investigates how these arrangements come about, but introductory chemistry is more interested in how many atoms of what type are in a particular kind of molecule.

When you know these things, you can predict what will happen when you manipulate chemicals, you can make other chemicals, and you can do many other interesting things!

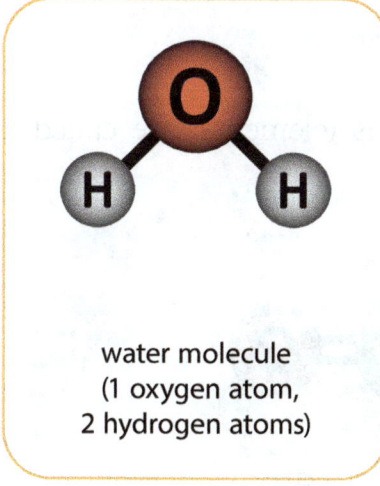

water molecule
(1 oxygen atom,
2 hydrogen atoms)

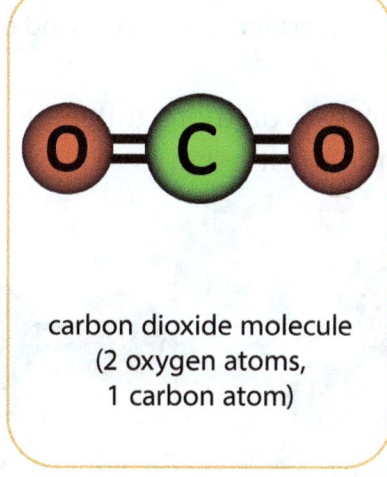

carbon dioxide molecule
(2 oxygen atoms,
1 carbon atom)

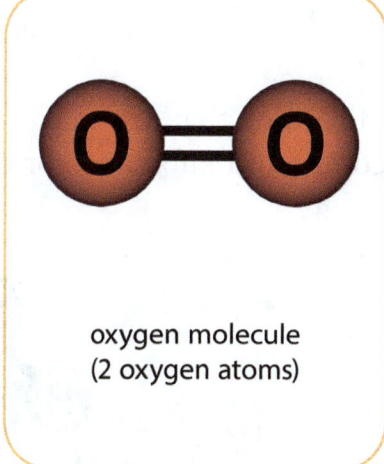

oxygen molecule
(2 oxygen atoms)

MOLECULES AND COMPOUNDS

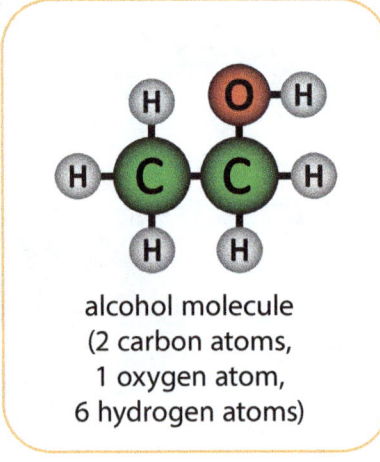

alcohol molecule
(2 carbon atoms,
1 oxygen atom,
6 hydrogen atoms)

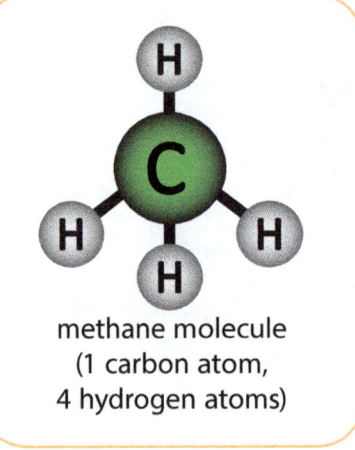

methane molecule
(1 carbon atom,
4 hydrogen atoms)

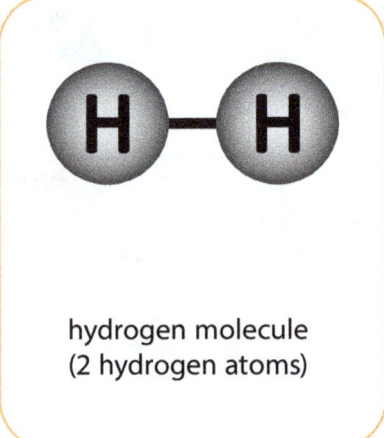

hydrogen molecule
(2 hydrogen atoms)

There is another thing about how atoms and molecules work that you need to know to do the activities in this book.

Molecules that are made up of only one kind of atom (element), such as hydrogen gas or oxygen gas, are called **elemental substances**. An elemental substance can also be a single atom, like iron.

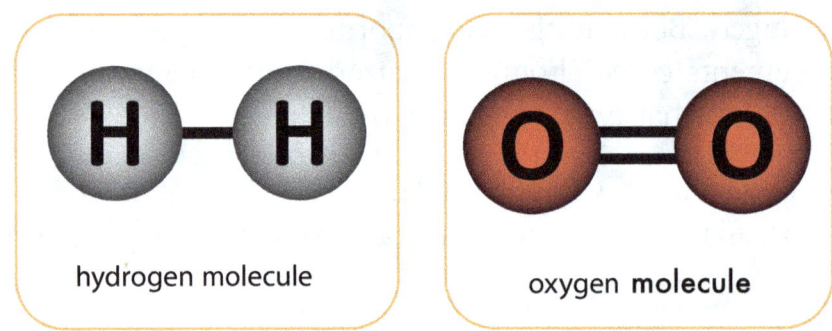

elemental substances (only one kind of atom)

Molecules that are made up of two or more different atoms (elements) are called a **compound substance** or **compound** for short.

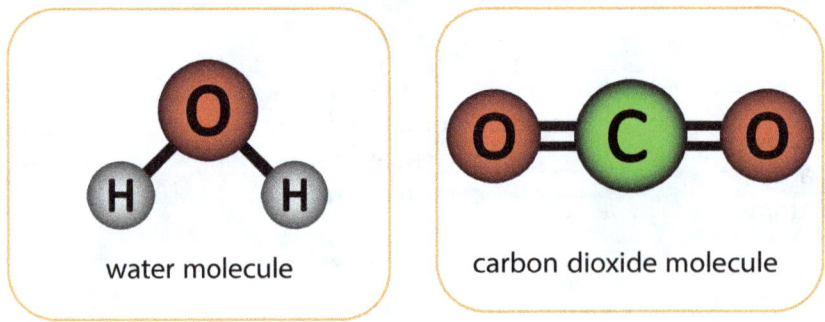

compound substances or compounds
(two or more different atoms)

MOLECULES AND COMPOUNDS

A chemical is a pure substance made up of only one kind of molecule, but can either be an elemental substance or a compound.

Because you can have so many combinations, there are of course many more compounds than there are elemental substances.

The word compound can refer to just one molecule or many, so whether you have one molecule of water or a gallon of water or a swimming pool full, it is still the compound called water.

The important thing about a chemical, a compound or an elemental substance is that all the molecules are the same. Most of the activities in this book work with elemental substances and compounds, but sometimes we will use mixtures (substances with various kinds of molecules) such as salt water or air.

Here are examples of compounds, some we have seen before, some new.

Water is a compound made of atoms of hydrogen and oxygen.

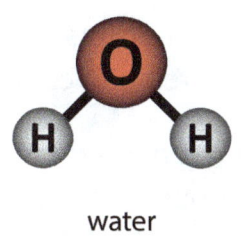

water

Carbon dioxide is a compound of carbon and oxygen.

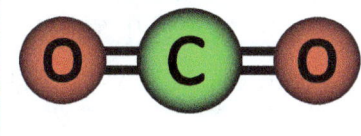

carbon dioxide

Alcohol is a compound of carbon, hydrogen and oxygen.

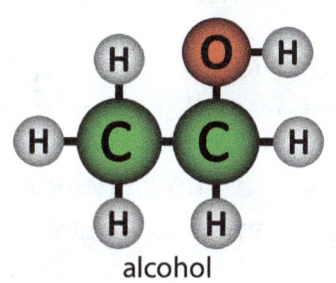

alcohol

Table salt is a compound of sodium (symbol Na) and chlorine (symbol Cl). (The symbol for sodium is Na because the Latin name for sodium is *natrium*.)

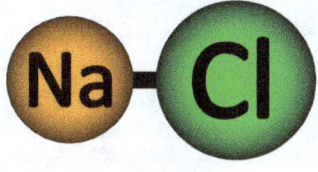

table salt

Baking soda is a compound of the elements sodium, carbon, hydrogen and oxygen.

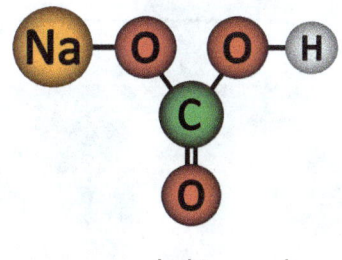

baking soda

MOLECULES AND COMPOUNDS

MIXTURES AND PURE SUBSTANCES

A chemical has just one kind of atom or molecule, so it is a pure substance. It has a definite structure. Mixtures like ice cream, soil, concrete, and even orange juice are much more complicated. The atoms, molecules and compounds are just mixed together.

Mixtures often can be separated out again into separate substances.

For example, if you dissolve sugar (a compound) in water (a compound), you get a mixture. The compounds are mixed together. But you can separate the sugar by evaporating the water. Now you have two pure substances again.

When the element iron is mixed with rock dust, you have a mixture. But you can separate the iron from the rock dust with a magnet.

Salt water is a mixture. But you can separate the salt by boiling off the water and collecting the water vapor.

Mixtures where the different molecules are *evenly* mixed with each other are called **solutions**. The molecules of the different ingredients are freely mixing together. Usually this applies to liquids, but air is an example of a solution that is a gas.

Other kinds of matter, which we could just call "stuff," are made of mixtures of pieces that are still in chunks or are mixed unevenly. Wood and concrete are good examples.

In all mixtures, including solutions, the compounds that are mixing remain themselves as compounds—they do not become transformed into other compounds.

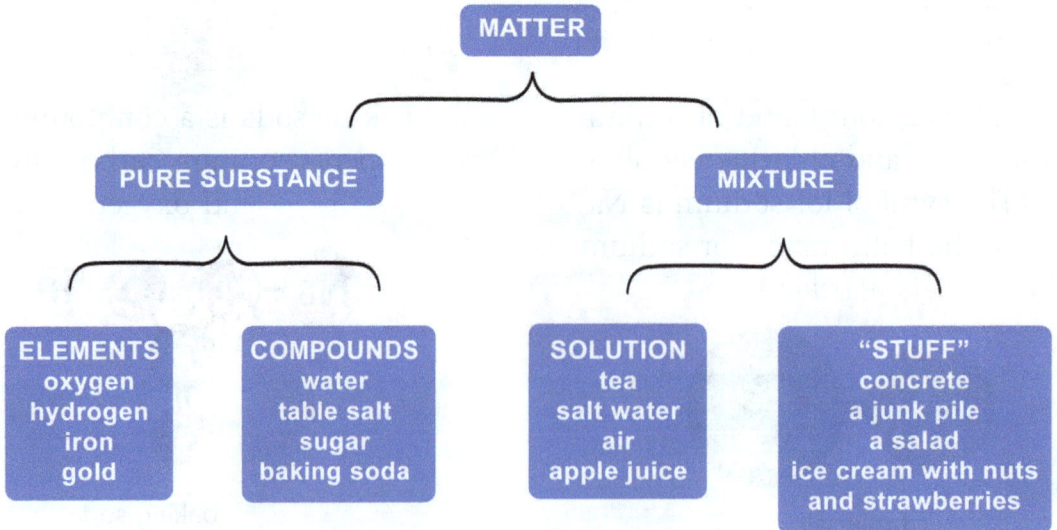

Chapter 6

Chemical Reactions

We now get to the main activity in chemistry—molecules interacting with other molecules and changing into different molecules.

A **chemical reaction** occurs when atoms and molecules actually combine (join) with each other or break apart, or both, so that different molecules, compounds and substances are formed. The new substances might be pure chemicals or mixtures.

Here is an example of a simple chemical reaction—one which you will actually perform later in the book:

hydrogen gas can combine with oxygen gas to form water.

In this case you are starting with two elemental substances and ending up with a compound. And in this case, you start with two gases and end up with a liquid.

This particular reaction can also be made to run in reverse—you can start with water and end up with hydrogen gas and oxygen gas. You will also get a chance to do this later in the book.

Remember the compound methane shown in chapter 5 with one carbon and four hydrogens?

methane molecule

It can combine in a chemical reaction with oxygen gas:

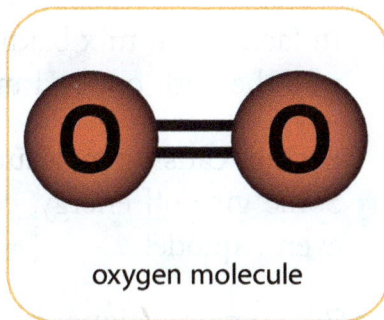
oxygen molecule

CHEMICAL REACTIONS

The atoms rearrange between the molecules and end up with these two compounds instead: water and carbon dioxide.

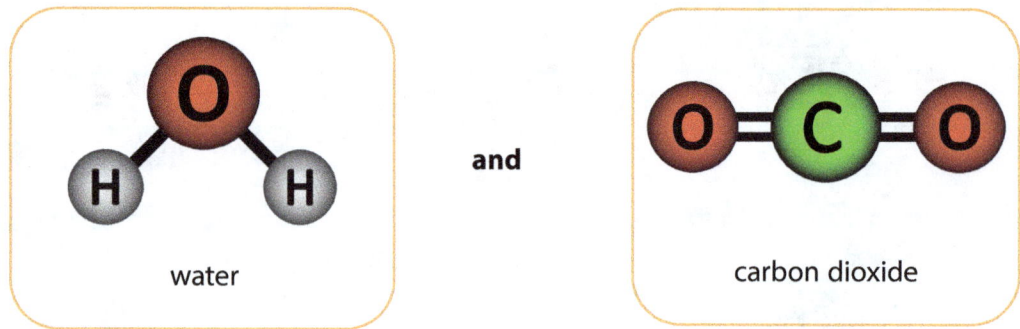

Notice in this example there aren't the same number of hydrogens and oxygens before and after the reaction. Of course that is not right—you have to end up with the same number of atoms that you started with—a reaction just rearranges the atoms in the molecules. As you go along in chemistry, you will learn how to show reactions like this more accurately. But this shows what the ingredients are and what the products are. (In chemistry, **products** are what is formed from a chemical reaction.)

Here is a fun reaction you will do frequently in chemistry. It is a reaction that you will find is easy to set up.

It starts with the ingredients:

baking soda and vinegar acid (two compounds)

and ends up with the products:

water, carbon dioxide and another more complex compound (three compounds).

When this happens, you get a lot of bubbles from the carbon dioxide that is formed.

In fact, if you mix baking soda and vinegar in a corked bottle, the carbon dioxide can pop the cork out and make it fly!

Besides causing molecules to change into other molecules, many reactions can happen. Some give off energy, commonly in the form of heat. So, the substances warm up or even explode!

But some reactions absorb energy, and in this case, the substances may cool off.

And some reactions are pretty neutral energy-wise. We will explore that more later.

ACTIVITY 2
Carbon Dioxide Cannon

For this activity, you will need:
- eye protection
- apron
- measuring cup
- white vinegar
- tablespoon
- baking soda
- cork or rubber stopper for bottle
- glass bottle (half-liter or less) used for carbonated drinks
- paper

Information:

In this activity, you will observe the chemical reaction that happens when the compounds baking soda and vinegar acid combine.

One of the products of the chemical reaction will be carbon dioxide gas.

And the pressure of the carbon dioxide gas will pop a stopper out of a bottle.

Steps:

1. Check to make sure the stopper fits the bottle well.

2. Put the jar in a sink.

3. Put on an apron and protective eye wear.

4. Fold the paper to make a crease and then unfold it.

5. Measure out about 2 tablespoons (66 grams) of baking soda onto the paper.

CHEMICAL REACTIONS

6. Pour the baking soda into the bottle using your creased paper.

7. Measure out half a cup of vinegar.

8. Very quickly pour the vinegar into the bottle, and stopper the bottle firmly, but not too tight.

9. Shake it once, then stand back and watch what happens. (Do not stand over the bottle or the stopper may hit you in the face.)

10. Pick up the stopper as quickly as you can and put it back in the bottle. See if there is enough gas still being produced to blow it out again.

Result:

The acid in the vinegar combines with the baking soda and creates a chemical reaction. It fizzes and bubbles, and carbon dioxide gas is produced.

The gas pressure builds up so fast inside the bottle that it blows out the stopper with a loud pop.

Chapter 7

Procedures

A **procedure** is a plan for doing something, often laid out in steps to follow.

In chemistry, when setting up and causing a chemical reaction, there is usually a procedure for doing it. Procedures help you run the reaction properly. And, very importantly, they help keep you safe. They also make it possible to repeat the reaction *the same way* if you need to.

Each activity in this book includes a procedure—a list of steps to do.

Here are some basic procedures you should learn because you will use them whether they are specifically mentioned in the activity or not. You need to be able to do these consistently and properly.

BASIC SAFETY

Put On an Apron

When you work with chemicals, always put on an apron. That will help keep your clothes clean and dry. Some chemicals can damage or stain cloth.

Wear Eye Glasses or Eye Protection

It is a good idea to wear glasses or eye protection when doing chemistry. *Always* wear eyewear if you are doing anything where there is a chance of something hitting you in the face, such as when working with flames or chemicals, or carefully pouring something.

When you must wear eye protection in this book, you will be told within the activity, but even so, it is always *your* job to ensure the safety of your eyes.

PROCEDURES

Wear Gloves

Reusable rubber gloves or single-use disposable gloves are useful for protecting your hands when dealing with certain chemicals. Most of the chemicals used in this book are not so strong that you must wear gloves, but you may choose to wear them anyway. When gloves are required, you will be told within the activity.

Where to Work

When you are dealing with chemicals or flames, the best place to work is on a counter and preferably alongside a sink. Depending on the activity, it may be best if the counter is fireproof and the kind that won't be damaged by chemicals.

Be sure to keep flame away from anything that could catch on fire. Also be sure there is good **ventilation** (circulation or change of air) so that you don't choke on smoke or fumes, or cause discomfort for others.

TWO SIMPLE PROCEDURES

Heating a Test Tube

When heating a test tube, there is always some chance of the contents spattering or the test tube shattering. So, when you heat a test tube, grip it with a test tube holder up near the open end.

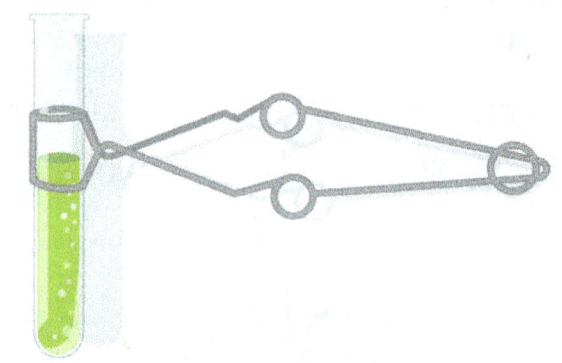

Hold it at a slant, ensuring that the mouth of the tube is pointed away from yourself and anyone else. Also always wear eye protection.

If the test tube is empty, heat it only briefly so the empty tube doesn't get too hot.

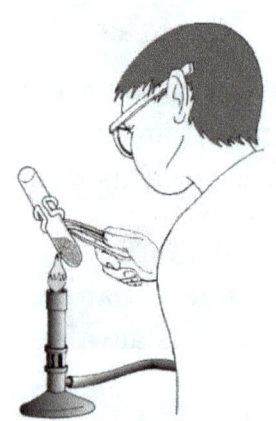

22

PROCEDURES

Pouring Powder

If you need to pour a powder into a container, some care is often needed to keep the powder under control. There are various ways to do that.

If you need a small amount of powder, crease a small piece of paper by folding it down the middle. Then place the powder on the center of the paper. To pour the powder, pick up the paper and tilt it so that the powder slides down the crease into the container.

If you need to pour powder into a container with a small opening, you can roll a sheet of paper into a cone shape and use it as a funnel.

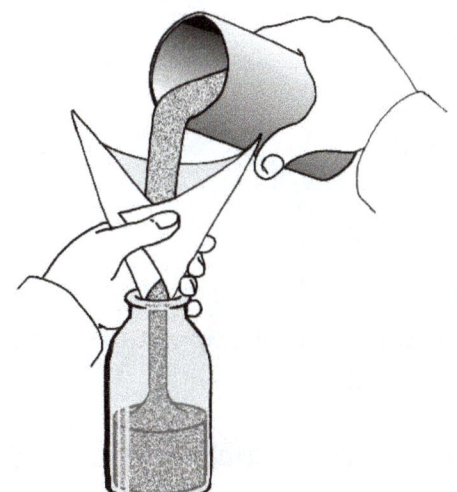

To make the paper hold its shape, hold it with your hand, or put a piece of tape across the edge of the sheet where it overlaps.

Insert the small end of the cone into the container and gently pour the powder into the cone. Pour a small amount at a time so the small end doesn't clog up. If it does, use something like a disposable coffee stirrer to break up the clog.

Another way is to use a funnel, if you have one.

23

PROCEDURES

ACTIVITY 3
Procedures Practice

For this activity, you will need:
- eye protection
- apron
- paper
- small mouth bottle
- table salt
- test tube
- glass or jar
- test tube holder
- burner

Procedure:

1. Practice pouring salt into a glass (or jar), using a creased piece of paper until you can do it without spilling any.

2. Practice pouring salt into a small-mouth bottle with a paper cone until you can do it without spilling any.

3. Using an empty test tube and a burner without a flame, go through the actions you would do to heat up a test tube, including putting on what you would wear.

4. Show your teacher your skills.

PROCEDURES

ACTIVITY 4
Grow Crystals of Sugar: Start

For this activity, you will need:
- large glass or jar—clear, heat-proof
- magnifying glass
- measuring cup
- tap water
- tape
- clean slender stick, such as a wood coffee stirer
- microwave oven
- dishwashing liquid
- waxed paper
- sugar
- teaspoon
- cloth or sponge

Information:

These are the steps you need to do ahead of time so that you have the results when you get to the activity later in the book.

Procedure:

1. Look at some grains of sugar with a magnifying glass. See if the grains tend to have a regular shape with some flat faces or not. Some crystals may have been crushed, but some may be intact.

2. Wet an inch or two of one end of the stick and roll it in sugar so that it is somewhat coated with sugar (this will be used to help your growing project get started). Set it aside to dry for about 20 minutes.

3. Put ½ cup water into a heat-proof large glass or jar and add 3/4 cup sugar.

25

PROCEDURES

4. Heat it in the microwave with occasional stirring until it is fully dissolved.

5. Add another 3/4 cup sugar and reheat, stirring as needed, until the liquid just begins to boil and the solution is clear again. It should be thick and syrup-like.

6. Take out a teaspoonful of the syrup and pour it onto a piece of waxed paper. Set it aside.

7. Use tape to position the stick from step 2 more or less vertically in the glass with the coated end in the sugar solution. The stick can rest on the bottom.

8. Set the glass and waxed paper away in a warm place where they will be undisturbed while they grow. Check them from time to time and look at them with the magnifying glass in bright light.

You will complete this on Activity 24 Grow Crystals of Sugar: Finish.

Special Cleanup:

Sugar is very sticky. Use a lot of water and a wet cloth or sponge to clean up any spills. To keep the surfaces from getting sticky, rinse out the cloth or sponge and clean the surfaces again with water and a little dishwashing liquid.

Chapter 8

Carbon and Candle Chemistry

Carbon is an element that is an important part of living cells. It is also part of some minerals and rocks. Carbon, by itself, is usually a blackish solid, as found in coal, or asphalt. Carbon compounds can be white, colored, clear or black.

The wax of a candle is made of carbon compounds, mostly long chains of carbon and hydrogen.

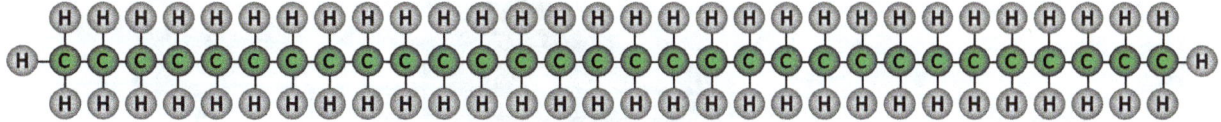

wax molecule
This molecule has 30 carbon atoms
and 62 hydrogen atoms.

When carbon compounds burn, that is a chemical reaction. In this reaction, carbon in the compound combines with oxygen from the air and produces the gas called carbon dioxide. The hydrogen in the compound combines with oxygen to form water.

We don't usually see the water because it comes out of the flame in the form of water vapor and goes off invisibly in the air.

Usually some soot is produced too. **Soot** is a black, greasy, powdery substance that is formed when fuels like wax, wood and oils are not burned up completely. The compounds in soot generally have some carbon left in them (i.e., that has not combined with oxygen), which is what makes them black.

CARBON AND CANDLE CHEMISTRY

When you bring a flame to a candle wick (to start the burning reaction), the first thing that happens is that some of the wax melts and spreads up through the wick. Then the heat of the flame causes that melted wax to turn into a vapor which catches on fire.

When the candle wax vapor catches on fire, the reaction combines the carbons and hydrogens in the wax with oxygen from the air and gives off energy in the form of light and heat.

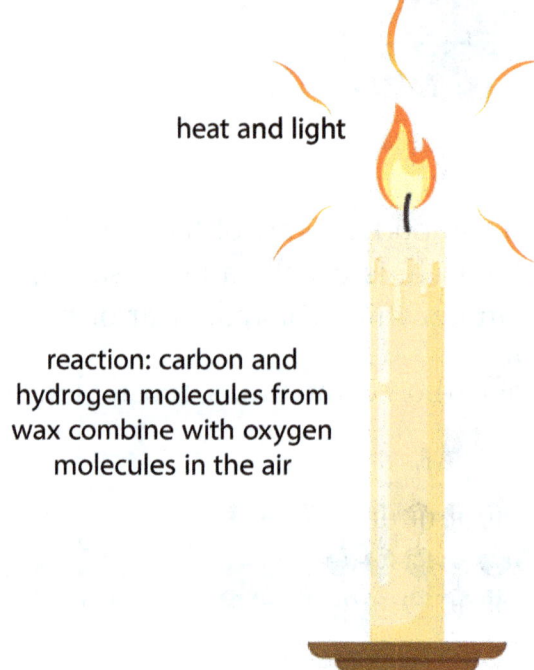

The chemical products are carbon dioxide (the carbons combine with oxygens) and water vapor (the hydrogens combine with oxygens). The heat causes some wax to continue melting, which travels up the wick to continue the flame.

If you blow out the flame, the candle wick still smokes for a little while. The smoke trail is wax vapor and other carbon compounds that haven't completely burned up.

Once the wax vapor is no longer being heated, it cools off rapidly and the smoke disappears. But the wax vapor does remain in the smoke near the wick for a moment. Do the next activity to see what happens when you touch a match to the smoke.

ACTIVITY 5
Candle Chemistry #1

For this activity, you will need:
- birthday candle
- small ball of clay
- wood splint (wooden coffee stirrer)
- matches or lighter

Procedure:

1. Use the ball of clay to hold the candle upright.

2. Light the candle and the wood splint (hold the splint in your hand).

3. Blow out the candle with a quick puff.

4. As soon as you see some smoke rising above the candle, bring the burning splint into the smoke about an inch above the candle and watch what happens.

Results:

The wax vapor in the smoke catches on fire again. This continues creating heat to melt the wax which continues supplying vapor so the candle catches on fire again.

CARBON AND CANDLE CHEMISTRY

ACTIVITY 6
Candle Chemistry #2

For this activity, you will need:

- candle
- matches or lighter
- aluminum foil—a small strip

Information:

We have learned that when you blow out the flame of a candle, the smoke trail from the wick is wax vapor and other carbon compounds that haven't completely burned up.

This activity shows the color of some of the carbon particles.

Procedure:

1. Light the candle.

2. Fold the strip of foil down the middle to make it stiffer.

3. Hold one end of the foil in the candle flame for a few seconds. Then remove it from the flame and look at it.

Results:

There will be a black, sooty smudge on the bottom side of the foil from the candle. Some of the compounds containing carbon atoms from the burning wax vapor stuck to the foil. These compounds did not complete the burning reaction before they hit the foil and stuck.

ACTIVITY 7
Candle Chemistry #3

For this activity, you will need:
- clay (small ball)
- birthday candle
- matches or lighter
- drinking glass (heat resistant) or beaker

Information:

Wax contains the elements hydrogen and carbon. When wax burns, carbon combines with oxygen from the air to form carbon dioxide, and hydrogen combines with oxygen from the air to form water vapor.

In this activity, we will see that water can be captured from the water vapor in a burning candle flame.

Procedure:

1. Make sure your beaker or glass is dry. If possible, first cool it. The cooler the glass you start with, the better this activity will work.
2. Stick a small ball of clay to a table.
3. Stick a birthday candle upright in the clay and light it.
4. Place the glass or beaker upside down over the candle and leave it there until the flame goes out.
5. Look to see whether there is moisture collecting on the inside of the glass/beaker.
6. Pick up the glass/beaker and feel the moisture on the inside with your finger.

Results:

A small amount of moisture should have collected on the glass. The moisture is water from the reaction of hydrogen in the wax with oxygen in the air to form water. The cooler the glass you start with, the better it will capture the water.

Chapter 9

Writing Chemical Reactions

Now that you have caused some chemical reactions, it's time to learn how chemists write them down.

There is a lot to keep track of when you're working with chemistry. You need to be able to keep track of what's happening for yourself, and also to communicate to others what occurred.

How this is done is actually kind of a "code." And now you are going to be one of the people who can write it and read it!

Let's start by reviewing the definition of "chemical reaction." A **chemical reaction** occurs when atoms and molecules actually combine (join) with each other or break apart, or both, so that different molecules, compounds and substances are formed. The new substances might be pure chemicals or mixtures.

So far we have shown a chemical reaction by drawing pictures of the different molecules and how they change during a reaction.

Here is a chemical reaction we mentioned earlier:

> The compound methane can combine with oxygen to form water and the compound carbon dioxide.

WRITING CHEMICAL REACTIONS

Here is a way to write down this chemical reaction using pictures. The arrow represents the reaction:

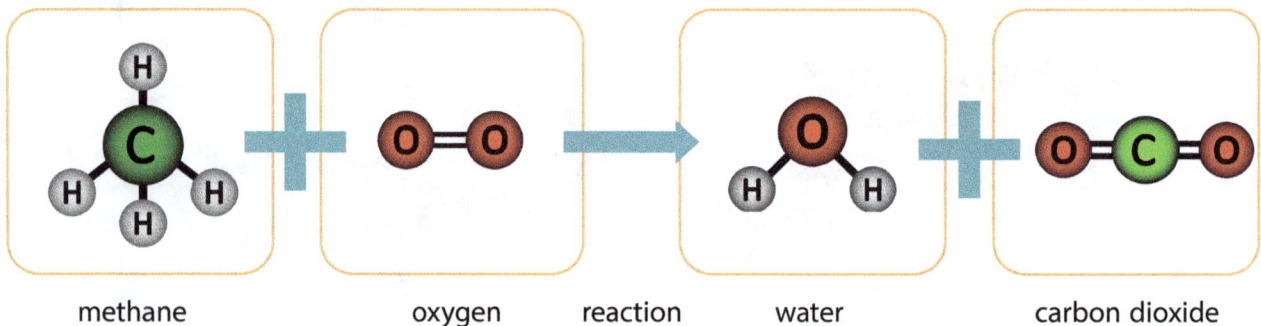

methane　　　　　oxygen　　reaction　　water　　　　carbon dioxide

This is very clear and you can see exactly what happened. But when you have a more complicated reaction with a lot of different elements, drawings like this don't work very well.

So here is the "code."

We've already shown that elements can be represented by symbols, like **O** for oxygen, **H** for hydrogen, **C** for carbon, **Na** for sodium, **Cl** for chlorine, and so on.

We can show chemical reactions by using these symbols to show compounds.

So, here we start with the symbols showing the ingredients, compound 1 and compound 2. We use the arrow to show the reaction. And then we show the symbols for the products, compound 3 and compound 4.

symbol 1 **+** symbol 2　　⟶　　symbol 3 **+** symbol 4
(reaction happens—the arrow means "produces")

You might start with 1, 2 or more compounds, and you might end up with 1, 2 or more compounds. The symbols tell you what atoms are involved in the molecules. And, as you'll see later, how many.

This way of showing a reaction is called a **reaction diagram**, and makes it easier to see what happens.

WRITING CHEMICAL REACTIONS

We will return to this after we understand better what the symbols are like, but here is a sneak preview. The symbols for methane and oxygen are **CH_4** and **O_2** and the symbols for water and carbon dioxide are **H_2O** and **CO_2**. The numerals tell you the number of atoms. Look at the pictures of these compounds to see how that works.

Now we can simplify our reaction diagram like this:

$$CH_4 \;+\; O_2 \;\longrightarrow\; H_2O \;+\; CO_2$$

We'll learn more later about making this more accurate, but now you know the basics of the code!

Chapter 10

Sugar and Carbon

Sugars are compounds that include carbon.

There are many kinds of sugars, and each one is made up of carbon, oxygen and hydrogen. The different kinds of sugar have different numbers of these elements or they are arranged differently.

Here are two examples of sugars that have different numbers of elements and are arranged differently:

The sugar you see most often is called table sugar or *sucrose*. The sucrose molecule has 12 carbon atoms, 22 hydrogen atoms, and 11 oxygen atoms.

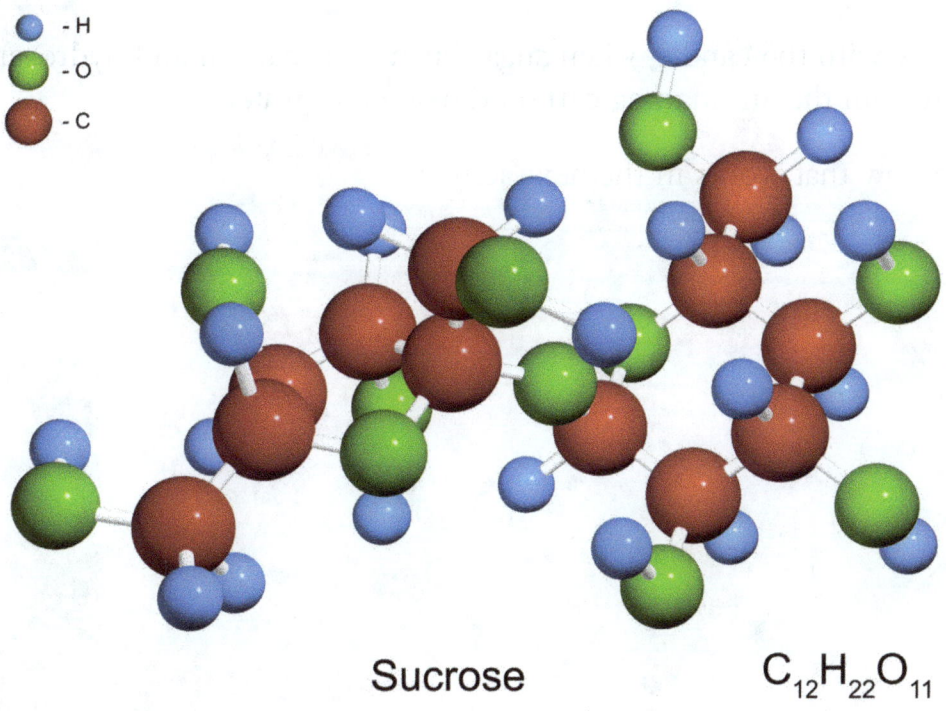

Sucrose $C_{12}H_{22}O_{11}$

SUGAR AND CARBON

Fruit sugar or *fructose* is simpler than sucrose. It has 6 carbon atoms, 12 hydrogen atoms and 6 oxygen atoms.

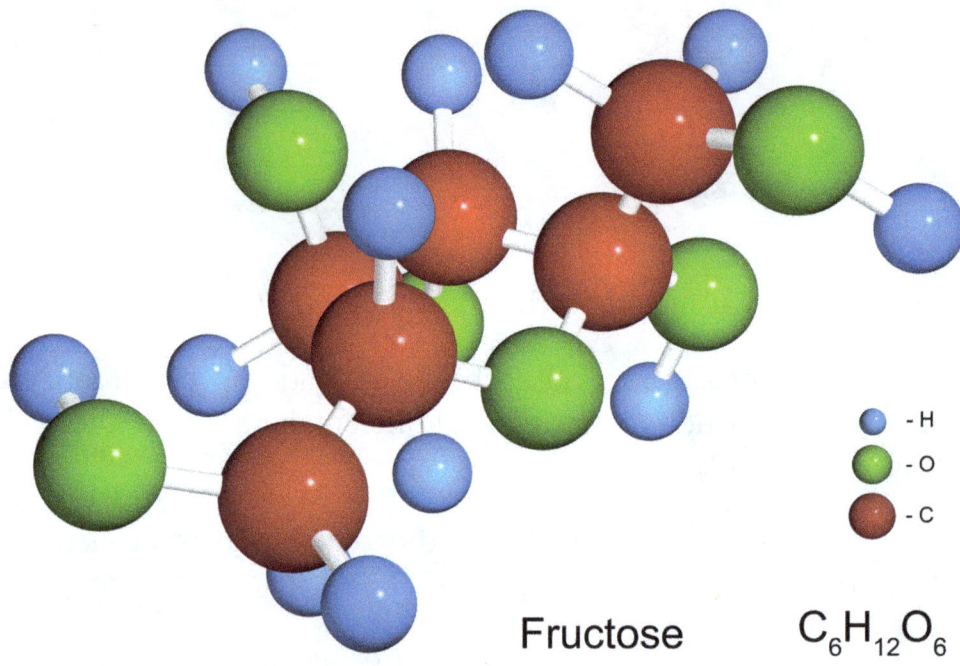

Fructose $C_6H_{12}O_6$

Just as we saw with the candle, when sugar burns, the carbon and hydrogen combine with oxygen from the air, making carbon dioxide and water.

We will see how that works in the next activity.

ACTIVITY 8
Burn a Sugar Cube

For this activity, you will need:
- apron
- eye protection
- sugar cubes
- 2 large squares of aluminum foil
- 2 candles that stand by themselves
- very small amount of potassium nitrate fertilizer (from garden store) (cigarette ash could also be used)
- matches or lighter
- paper towels
- tongs or large tweezers

Information:

Like wax, sugar will burn, but it takes longer to get the burning reaction started, and it does not burn evenly.

In this activity, you will be burning sugar. Because the sugar by itself would not burn very well, another compound is added to it and together they burn much better.

We will see that when sugar burns, the carbon and hydrogen combine with oxygen from the air, making carbon dioxide and water.

Procedure:

1. Place one candle upright on a large square of aluminum foil (you need a surface where it is okay to drip melting or burning sugar). Place a small pile of potassium nitrate nearby on a square of foil. Place the second candle nearby.

2. Put on your apron and eye protection, and light both candles.

SUGAR AND CARBON

3. With tweezers, hold a sugar cube in the flame of the first candle until an edge melts.

4. Dip the melted edge in potassium nitrate powder. (As noted, this compound will help the burning reaction start and cause the sugar cube to burn instead of just melting.)

5. Hold the sugar cube just above the flame until the sugar cube catches on fire.

6. Move the sugar cube away from the flame when it starts burning but keep it over a dish or foil because melted sugar will drip and is very messy and very hot. If the flame goes out, use the second candle to re-light it.

Results:

When the sugar cube catches on fire (when the reaction starts) at step 4, at first it burns with a blue flame, bubbles and produces little puffs of smoke. As the sugar cube continues to burn, it melts and turns black.

The black comes from carbon that has not combined with oxygen and is left over, but much of the sugar has reacted with oxygen from the air and produced carbon dioxide gas, water and other compounds. The puffs are from pockets of carbon dioxide bursting.

Chapter 11

Oxygen and Its Reactions

Oxygen gas is colorless and has no taste, and you breathe it every minute of every day. When you breathe in oxygen, it takes part in chemical reactions in your body.

The process in which oxygen combines with other kinds of atoms or molecules is called **oxidation**. Oxidation is very common and happens all around us all the time.

As you learned in the last two chapters, if you burn a candle or sugar, carbon combines with oxygen in the air and forms a gas called carbon dioxide. That is oxidation. We say the carbon got *oxidized*. The same thing would happen if you burned paper or wood or other things that contain carbon.

You may have noticed that the oxidation reactions you produced gave off heat. Many, but not all, oxidation reactions give off energy in the form of heat. And, as you have seen, some also give off light.

In most kinds of burning reactions, a substance reacts chemically with oxygen to form some new compounds. If there isn't much left after burning, that is because most of the compounds formed were gases that tended to float away.

Here are some other oxidation reactions:

- Rust is the result of oxygen combining with iron.
- If hydrogen reacts with oxygen, the combination gives you water.
- When you eat food, it combines with oxygen in your body and is oxidized. In these reactions, the oxidation of the food chemicals makes new compounds that your body uses for growth and energy. These are oxidation reactions that give off energy in the form of heat, which is how our bodies stay warm.

OXYGEN AND ITS REACTIONS

Like nearly all living things, human bodies must have oxygen to live.

You might be interested to know that air is a mixture of different kinds of gas molecules—it is about 1/5 oxygen. It breaks down this way:

78.0% nitrogen gas	Nitrogen gas is transparent and odorless and usually isn't involved in burning. Normally we just breathe it in and out.
20.9% oxygen gas	Some of the oxygen we breathe in is captured by the body and gets involved in oxidation reactions.
0.9% argon gas	Argon gas (also transparent and odorless) does not react with anything. Because of this, it is used inside light bulbs instead of air so they will last longer (if there is no oxygen in the light bulb, the filament can't oxidize and get destroyed).
0.2% all other gases together (a very tiny amount)	This includes **water vapor** (invisible gaseous water), which is 0.05% of the air and carbon dioxide gas, which is 0.04% of the air. Carbon dioxide is produced by many oxidation reactions, including in our bodies—we breathe it out. Carbon dioxide is absolutely essential for plant growth.

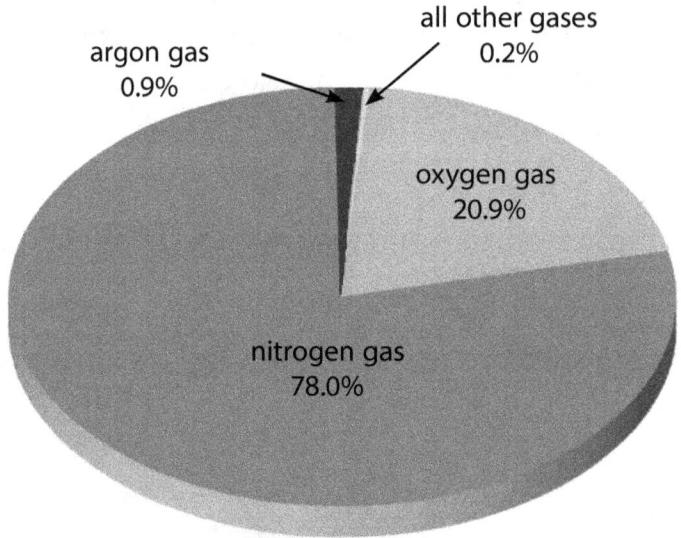

ACTIVITY 9
Use Up Oxygen with Fire

For this activity, you will need:
- bowl
- plastic bottle—500 ml or larger with lid
- knife
- short candle
- food coloring
- matches or lighter
- tap water
- 1-inch ball of clay

Information:

This activity shows that quite a bit of the air is oxygen.

Procedure:

0. Cut the bottom out of the bottle making sure it will still stand upright. Remove the cap but keep it nearby.

1. Stick the candle to the bottom of the bowl with a 1-inch ball of clay.

2. Pour about 1½ inch of water into the bowl (don't get the candle wick wet). Add a few drops of food coloring.

3. Light the candle.

4. Put the bottle down over the candle so it is standing in the bottom of the bowl in the water and *quickly* screw the cap on.

5. Watch what happens. When the candle goes out, compare the water level in the bottle with the water level in the bowl. You may need to wait a few minutes while the gas in the bottle cools off.

OXYGEN AND ITS REACTIONS

Results:

The oxygen in the bottle gets "used up" as candle wax and oxygen react (burn) to make carbon dioxide and water. Of course, it isn't really used up—it is now in these other two compounds.

Together these compounds take up less space than the oxygen did originally, so there is less gas in the bottle than there was originally. The outside air then pushes water up into the bottle to replace the missing oxygen gas.

You may have to wait a few minutes because the candle may have heated the air in the bottle and made it expand. When it cools off, that expansion goes away.

ACTIVITY 10
Make Writing Disappear

For this activity, you will need:
- apron
- eye protection
- disposable gloves
- permanent marker
- ballpoint pen with blue ink
- liquid chlorine bleach
- highlighter
- paper—1 sheet
- cotton swab like a Q-tip

Information:

Chlorine bleach is a chemical compound that includes oxygen, sodium and chlorine.

When cloth is bleached, it is often exposed to a weak solution of the bleach, and the oxygen in the bleach reacts with compounds in the colored stains and turns them into colorless compounds.

Because bleach can cause oxidation with many substances (including skin), it has to be handled carefully. If too strong a solution is used on cloth, it can cause damage by oxidizing the cloth itself.

Procedure:

Handle the bleach carefully, and wear good protection.

1. Make a few marks on a sheet of paper with a permanent marker, a blue ballpoint pen and a highlighter.

2. Put on an apron, disposable gloves and eye protection.

OXYGEN AND ITS REACTIONS

3. Arrange a small amount of bleach so you can easily get your swab into it without touching the bleach yourself.

4. Swab bleach on parts of each of the three different kinds of marks.

5. Wait about 5 minutes, then look at the marks. Notice if there is any difference in what the bleach did to each mark.

6. Dispose of the bleach and paper carefully.

Results:

The oxygen in the bleach has oxidized the ink molecules and caused them to fade or lose their colors. The bleached highlighter color should have mostly disappeared, and the ballpoint pen and marker colors should be lighter after a few minutes.

Chapter 12

Oxidizing Iron

Maybe you have seen a rusty car or a rusty bicycle that had been left outside for a long time.

Chemistry can tell you why that happens.

It starts with the element, iron. Iron makes up about 5% of the earth's crust and is the cheapest metal for building things.

Pure iron is not very strong so small amounts of other elements are added in with it to make a much stronger metal (mixture) called *steel*.

When oxygen from the air combines with iron or with the iron in steel, this oxidation reaction forms solid rust, which is usually reddish-brown. Rust is a kind of compound called iron oxide.

Dry iron rusts very slowly, but wet iron rusts much faster unless it is protected with paint or some other coating.

An even faster way to oxidize iron is by burning it.

You can't burn large pieces of iron or steel easily, but if iron or steel is cut up into fine enough pieces, it will burn. That is because when the pieces are very fine, there is much more metal surface for the oxygen molecules to get to. This makes it much easier for the oxygen molecules to combine with the iron atoms (in other words, for the iron to get oxidized).

In the next activities, you will oxidize iron by creating rust and by burning it.

OXIDIZING IRON

ACTIVITY 11
Produce Rust

For this activity, you will need:
- steel wool pad (not soaped) "0000" steel wool pad is the thinnest and works best.
- test tube
- glass or jar
- warm water

Information:

Steel wool is nearly all iron. In this activity you can see the effects of oxygen in the air reacting with iron in steel wool to form rust.

Procedure:

1. Pull a few pieces off the steel wool pad until you have an amount about the size of a quarter, then stretch it out.

2. Put the steel wool pieces inside a test tube and push them to the bottom with a pencil or something long.

3. Wet the steel wool with warm water and then pour off the water.

4. Fill the glass (or jar) with about an inch of warm water and stand the tube upside down in it (you can let a little water into the mouth of the tube so it stands up well).

5. Wait overnight and check the test tube again. Notice where the water level is now, and check for any rusting.

Results:

Overnight the water level rises about 1/5 of the way up the tube, and you can see spots of rust on the steel wool.

Water rises in the test tube because most of the oxygen in the air has gone through the oxidation reaction with the iron to make solid rust.

The rust compound forms on the steel wool and takes up much less room than the oxygen gas and iron did before. That leaves more room inside the test tube, so the outside air pushes water into the test tube to fill the space.

Water is pushed about 1/5 of the way into the tube because air is about 1/5 oxygen and nearly all the oxygen has been removed from the air. (If the water doesn't rise 1/5 of the way up, the reaction requires more time.)

OXIDIZING IRON

ACTIVITY 12
Burn Iron

For this activity, you will need:
- steel wool pad (not soaped)
- tongs or large tweezers
- candle
- protective eye wear
- apron
- clay ball
- access to sink or fireproof surface
- matches or lighter

Procedure:

Work in a sink or on a surface that won't burn.

1. Pull out some strands of steel wool and fluff them up to about the size of a baseball.

2. Use the ball of clay to stick the candle in the bottom of the sink (or other fireproof surface). Don't let the candle get wet.

3. Put on an apron and protective eye wear.

4. Light the candle.

5. Hold the steel wool in the flame with tongs or large tweezers until the steel wool starts burning.

6. Lift the steel wool away from the candle flame, but keep it above the sink or other fireproof surface, and watch what happens.

Results:

The steel wool will heat up, glow, burn, sputter and send off sparks.

Procedure (continued):

7. After the sparks go out, try to burn the steel wool again and watch what happens.

Results:

The steel wool won't burn any more or burns poorly, and hard drops of material may form from the melted metal.

The iron has been oxidized, but the new material formed is not rust and it won't burn. It is another kind of iron oxide called *hematite*. This is the kind of iron oxide that is common on the planet Mars. It's what gives Mars a reddish look.

Chapter 13

More About Writing Chemical Reactions

Are you ready for more code?

We have learned that all elements have symbols. The names are often but not always taken from the English name for the element, like **H** for hydrogen, **O** for oxygen, **He** for helium, etc. Some elements get their symbol from names in other languages, like **Na** for sodium (*natrium* in Latin) or **Cu** for copper (*cuprum* in Latin).

When atoms combine to make a molecule, the molecule gets its code name from the symbols of the atoms. This name is called a **formula** because it tells both what atoms and how many of each kind are there. Here are two simple examples.

A water molecule consists of two hydrogen atoms, both linked to an oxygen atom.

The formula for a water molecule is written as **H₂O** (pronounced "H 2 O"). The subscript ₂ tells you that in each water molecule there are 2 hydrogen atoms. (*Sub* means below and *script* means writing.)

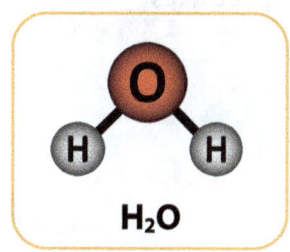

If you wanted to indicate that two water molecules were involved, you would put a 2 out front: **2H₂O**.

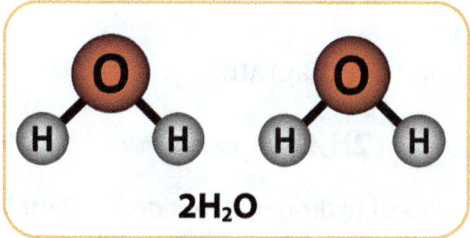

53

MORE ABOUT WRITING CHEMICAL REACTIONS

Hydrogen peroxide is a compound that also consists of hydrogen and oxygen, but a hydrogen peroxide molecule has an extra oxygen atom and is written **H_2O_2**.

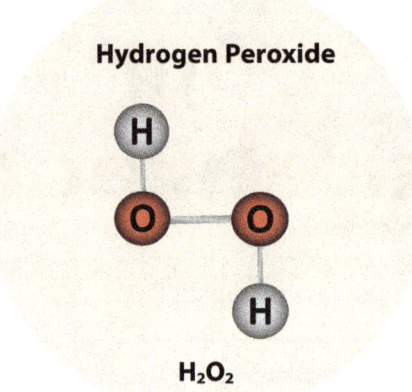

A simple kind of reaction that hydrogen peroxide can have is to break down into smaller molecules. When hydrogen peroxide breaks down (or decomposes), it forms water and oxygen gas.

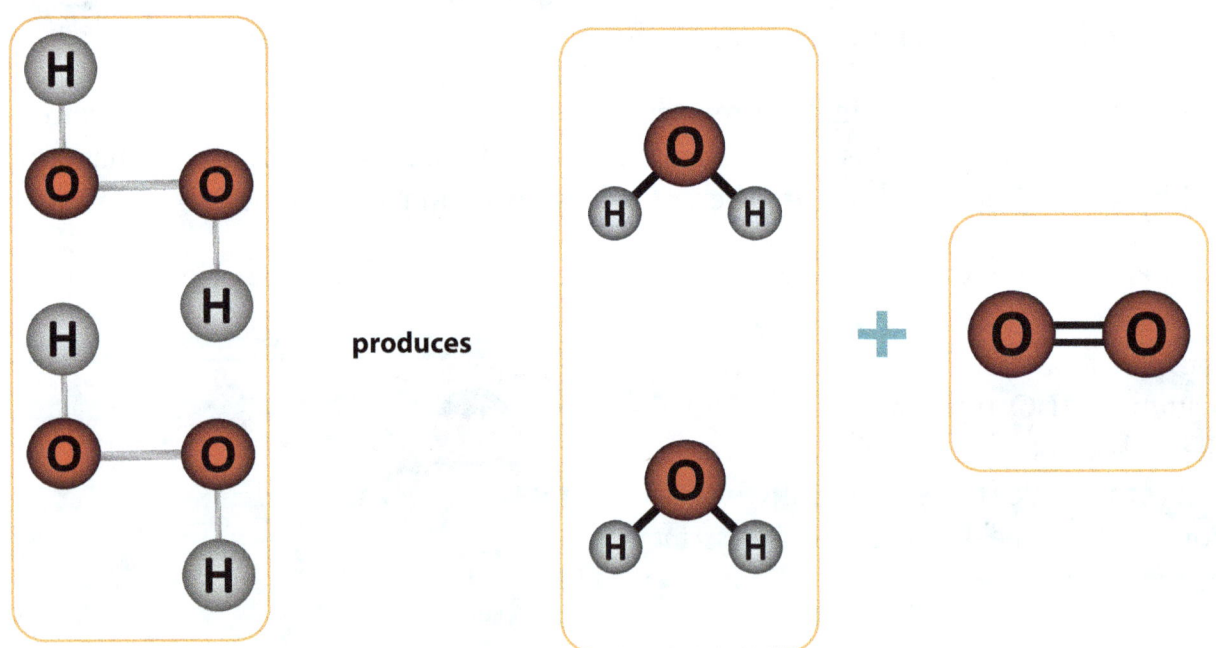

Here is its reaction diagram:

2 molecules of hydrogen peroxide — 2 molecules of water and one molecule of oxygen gas
(4 hydrogen atoms and 4 oxygen atoms)   (4 hydrogen atoms and 4 oxygen atoms)

Notice that in this reaction there are the same numbers of atoms on both sides of the arrow, before and after the reaction. This kind of balance is true of all chemical reactions, and it is important that reaction diagrams are balanced in this way.

Chapter 14

Using Hydrogen Peroxide to Produce Oxygen

In the last chapter, we talked about how hydrogen peroxide breaks down (or decomposes) to form water and oxygen gas.

When hydrogen peroxide breaks down like this, oxygen gas appears as foamy gas bubbles in the water, which then can combine with many other substances and oxidize them.

This ability to easily produce oxygen makes hydrogen peroxide very useful for many things, as we will see. An everyday use is for cleaning wounds and cleaning rooms, because the oxygen goes to work oxidizing things and this kills germs.

CATALYSTS

There are some chemicals, called **catalysts**, which help reactions between other compounds without themselves getting used up. Catalysts are sort of active "spectators" to the reaction—they encourage it but don't actually get involved. This is easy to demonstrate when working with hydrogen peroxide.

Normally hydrogen peroxide is clear like water, and will stay stable when left alone in a bottle. In other words, it doesn't have the decomposing reaction. But many substances carry a chemical catalyst that will cause hydrogen peroxide to immediately decompose, with the release of heat and bubbles of oxygen gas.

USING HYDROGEN PEROXIDE TO PRODUCE OXYGEN

You can think of a catalyst as triggering and helping a reaction but not really getting caught up in the reaction. In the next activity, you will use yeast cells to decompose hydrogen peroxide. This works because the yeast cells contain compounds that act as catalysts for hydrogen peroxide, **H_2O_2**.

Yeast cells are living organisms. And many living organisms have catalysts in their cells that will cause hydrogen peroxide to break down. Hydrogen peroxide is poisonous to cells, so organisms probably developed these catalysts as a way to protect themselves by breaking the peroxide down.

When hydrogen peroxide is used to clean up a wound, compounds in the blood act as a catalyst and cause it to foam with oxygen and give off heat.

Once hydrogen peroxide (often just called peroxide) gets catalyzed, the reaction runs very fast and produces quite a bit of heat. So, it has to be diluted before it is safe to handle. (**Dilute** means make a chemical weaker by adding water.)

When you buy it at a drugstore, the bottle usually contains only 3% peroxide. This is safe as long as you take care to keep it away from your eyes.

You can get stronger peroxide from a hair salon, where it is used for bleaching and coloring hair. This is about 6% hydrogen peroxide. (It may be labeled 20 *vol* hydrogen peroxide, which is a measure of how much oxygen gas it will release.)

90% hydrogen peroxide reacts so strongly and produces so much gas that it is used as a rocket fuel!

USING HYDROGEN PEROXIDE TO PRODUCE OXYGEN

ACTIVITY 13
Elephant's Toothpaste

For this activity, you will need:

- apron
- eye protection
- dishwashing liquid
- food coloring
- measuring cup
- matches or lighter
- sink or tray
- warm water
- teaspoon
- tablespoon
- plastic soda bottle—16 oz, or half-liter
- cup
- dry yeast (15 grams or 1 tablespoon)
- hydrogen peroxide—6% (from hair dresser) or 3% from drugstore
- sponge

Information:

This activity is called Elephant's Toothpaste because the foam produced looks like toothpaste coming out of a giant tube that is big enough for an elephant!

You can use either 3% or 6% hydrogen peroxide in this activity, but you will find the 6% version makes a better show.

USING HYDROGEN PEROXIDE TO PRODUCE OXYGEN

Procedure:

Reminder: Either strength of hydrogen peroxide is strong enough to harm your eyes if splashed into them. You should do this activity carefully and under the supervision of an adult.

1. Put on an apron and eye protection.

2. Measure ½ cup of hydrogen peroxide into the measuring cup and carefully pour it into the bottle.

3. Place the bottle in the sink or tray.

4. Add several drops of a food coloring to the bottle.

5. Add 2 teaspoons of dishwashing liquid to the bottle and swish the bottle around a bit to mix it.

6. In a separate small cup, combine 100 ml or 1/3 cup of warm water and 1 tablespoon or packet of yeast (15 grams) and stir together for about 30 seconds.

7. Quickly pour the yeast water mixture into the bottle.

8. Watch what happens and feel the bottle.

Results:

The catalyst produced by the yeast cells causes hydrogen peroxide to break down into oxygen and water. The peroxide begins to foam immediately and continues to produce oxygen foam out of the bottle for some minutes. The oxygen gas is trapped in bubbles because of the dishwashing liquid. This happens very fast and creates lots of bubbles and releases lots of heat.

The foam produced is just water, detergent, and oxygen so you can clean it up with a sponge and carefully pour any extra liquid left in the bottle down the drain.

USING HYDROGEN PEROXIDE TO PRODUCE OXYGEN

MORE HYDROGEN PEROXIDE ACTIVITIES

Additional materials—if you choose to do all the activities, you will need:

- 3% hydrogen peroxide, (if 6% was used previously, or 6% if 3% was used previously)
- a different type of dishwashing liquid
- match or lighter
- old washcloth
- slice of apple, potato or another vegetable
- Manganese dioxide (**MnO$_2$**), sodium iodide (**NaI**) or potassium iodide (**KI**)

Activities:

Here you will do Activity 13, varying it as directed.

☐ If you use 3% hydrogen peroxide to make elephant's toothpaste, does it actually produce a lot less foam than 6%? If you used 6% the first time you did the Elephant's Toothpaste activity, try it now with 3% hydrogen peroxide.

☐ Does it make any difference if you use a different dishwashing liquid? Try doing the Elephant's Toothpaste activity with a different dishwashing liquid and see.

☐ The bubbles in the elephant's toothpaste are full of oxygen gas. Will they make a flame burn brighter? Make elephant's toothpaste, light a match or lighter, and hold it near the foam (but don't touch it or let the match get wet).

☐ Will the foam be different if you don't add dishwashing liquid to the hydrogen peroxide solution? Will you get any foam at all? Try doing the Elephant's Toothpaste activity without adding dishwashing liquid to the hydrogen peroxide solution and see. Was the foam different? Did you get any foam at all?

☐ Try pouring some peroxide on a slice of apple, potato or another vegetable and you will see how the catalysts in their cells cause some oxygen bubbles from the breakdown of peroxide.

☐ Try pouring some of the hydrogen peroxide solution on an old washcloth. It may foam and bubble if a chemical whitener was used the last time the cloth was washed and some of the chemical stayed on the cloth. The chemical whitener acts as a catalyst to make the hydrogen peroxide break down to water and oxygen.

USING HYDROGEN PEROXIDE TO PRODUCE OXYGEN

☐ Manganese dioxide (MnO_2) is another example of a catalyst, as are sodium iodide (**NaI**) and potassium iodide (**KI**). If you have one or more of these, you could repeat the Elephant's Toothpaste activity and substitute one of them for yeast. How do they work compared to the yeast?

Chapter 15

Carbon Dioxide

CARBON DIOXIDE IN THE AIR

Carbon dioxide gas makes up only 0.04% of the air, but it is a chemical that is very important to living things. It is a basic building block for making food.

Green plants take carbon dioxide gas from the air and combine it with water to make compounds that contain carbon atoms, such as sugar, starch and other compounds that plants use to grow. (We will explore this in an activity later.)

By capturing carbon from the air this way, plants start the formation of just about all the food on the planet. Plants die and other plants are fertilized by the carbon from the dead plants. Animals eat the plants and grow. Other animals eat those animals. The carbon compounds just keep moving on to other living creatures, including humans.

We already know that nearly all life on Earth depends on oxygen. Now you can see that it also depends on carbon dioxide to feed the plants.

CARBON DIOXIDE IN ROCKS

You might be surprised to know that most of the carbon dioxide in the world is not in the atmosphere but is tied up in minerals in rocks. There is more carbon dioxide in rocks than in all the air, soil and sea combined!

Carbon dioxide can be released from a rock by treating it with an **acid**—a substance that has a sour, sharp or biting taste. An acid molecule has one or more hydrogen atoms (H) that are held loosely and are free to react with other atoms or molecules. Vinegar, lemon juice and orange juice all contain acids, but most acids are not foods and many are poisonous.

Carbonates are rocks, minerals and chemical compounds whose molecules have carbon and oxygen in them, and which react with acids to release carbon dioxide. Carbonates are common in rocks from the sea and in seashells. If you pour acid on a rock containing a carbonate, it will react with the carbonate part of the rock and release carbon dioxide gas, often with a fizzing sound. The gas will come off slowly or fast, depending on the type of material.

If you add vinegar to a powder that contains carbonate, the reaction will go much faster because the powder has much more surface area for the acid to reach and react with.

We will next explore ways of producing and using carbon dioxide.

CARBON DIOXIDE

ACTIVITY 14
Release Carbon Dioxide from Antacid Tablets

For this activity, you will need:

- antacid tablets that contain calcium carbonate (2)
- beakers, glasses or jars (2)
- vinegar
- hammer

Information:

Most antacid tablets provide a handy source of carbonates (and some other minerals). There is acid in the stomach, and sometimes it is desired to reduce the amount of that acid. When these tablets are swallowed, the carbonate reacts with the stomach acid and reduces it (antacid = anti-acid). Of course, in the process carbon dioxide is produced. This activity demonstrates this with antacid tablets that contain the mineral, calcium carbonate.

Procedure:

1. Place an antacid tablet in the first glass.

2. Break up a second antacid into tiny pieces or powder and put it in the second glass.

3. Fill both glasses about 1/4 full with vinegar. Then watch what happens.

Results:

In the first glass, carbon dioxide gas slowly bubbles off the surface of the tablet.

Bubbles form much more rapidly in the second glass where the tablet has been broken into small pieces because the vinegar can get to more surface. Antacid tablets also contain some other compounds that don't react with vinegar, so some pieces of the tablet might not dissolve.

Chapter 16

Putting Carbon Dioxide to Work

CARBON DIOXIDE GAS EXPANDS

When carbon and other atoms are locked up in carbonate molecules in rocks, they are part of a solid and take up very little space. But when there is a chemical reaction and carbon dioxide gas is formed, it expands to fill up a lot more space. This can be very useful.

Baking soda is a carbonate which is used to make some kinds of pastry or dough expand ("rise"). This works because when it reacts with other chemicals in the dough, it produces tiny bubbles of carbon dioxide that push the dough up and out.

We have already seen what happens when the acid in vinegar reacts with baking soda. So much carbon dioxide is released all at once that the gas can build up and create a strong pressure if it is inside a closed container. And that pressure can be used to throw things quite a distance.

It is the same kind of thing that happens when a bullet is fired. When gunpowder is exploded inside a gun, hot gas is produced. The gas expands so fast that it makes a loud noise and can push a bullet out the barrel at high speed.

CARBON DIOXIDE CHOKES OUT FIRE

If you have a jar sitting on the counter and you hold a burning match just inside the top of the jar, the flame continues to burn. But if, instead of being full of air, your jar is full of carbon dioxide, and you hold that same burning match inside the top of the jar, the match goes out immediately.

Carbon dioxide gas is heavier than other air molecules, so if you can get a jar full of it, it will stay there, just like water stays in a jar.

Now why does it put the match out?

We know that oxygen must be present for a match to burn. But when oxygen is combined with carbon in carbon dioxide gas (CO_2), the oxygen is not free to combine with other atoms and cause them to burn. As a result, carbon dioxide gas can starve a fire by cutting off the supply of oxygen.

Of course, there are other ways to put out fire, such as cooling it off with water. The problem is that water doesn't always work, like on an oil fire where the burning oil can simply float on the water. And sometimes the water itself can cause damage, like in an electrical fire. Carbon dioxide, by starving all kinds of fire of oxygen, avoids some of these problems.

Many fire extinguishers are made using carbon dioxide because it flows and sinks and does not burn.

PUTTING CARBON DIOXIDE TO WORK

ACTIVITY 15
Carbon Dioxide Cannon (Repeat)

For this activity, you will need:
- apron
- eye protection
- white vinegar
- tablespoon
- baking soda
- cork or rubber stopper for bottle
- measuring cup
- paper
- glass bottle (half-liter or less) used for carbonated drinks

Information:

This activity is repeated here, in case you would like to do it again now that you know more about what is happening with these reactions.

In this activity you can use the pressure of carbon dioxide gas to pop a stopper out of a bottle.

Procedure:

1. Check to make sure the stopper fits the bottle well.
2. Put the jar in a sink.
3. Put on an apron and protective eye wear.
4. Fold the paper to make a crease and then unfold it.
5. Measure out about 2 tablespoons (66 grams) of baking soda onto the paper.
6. Pour the baking soda into the bottle using your creased paper.

PUTTING CARBON DIOXIDE TO WORK

7. Measure out half a cup of vinegar.

8. Very quickly pour the vinegar into the bottle, and stopper the bottle firmly, but not too tight.

9. Shake it once, then stand back and watch what happens. (Do not stand over the bottle or the stopper may hit you in the face.)

10. Pick up the stopper as quickly as you can and put it back in the bottle. See if there is enough gas still being produced to blow it out again.

Result:

The acid in the vinegar reacts with the baking soda and fizzes and bubbles. Carbon dioxide is released into the bottle and after a few seconds the stopper will blow out with a loud pop. The gas pressure builds up so fast inside the bottle that it blows out the stopper.

ACTIVITY 16
Carbon Dioxide Fire Extinguisher #1

For this activity, you will need:
- jar or glass—large
- measuring cup
- wooden matches
- baking soda
- vinegar
- tablespoon

Procedure:

1. Light a wooden match and hold it just inside the jar (or glass). Notice what happens to the flame.

Results:

It continues to burn because air is in the jar.

Procedure (continued):

2. Blow out the match.

3. Put a tablespoon of baking soda (33 grams) in the jar.

4. Add ¼ cup of vinegar. (The baking soda will fizz.)

5. Immediately light another match and hold it just inside the jar. Notice what happens to the flame this time.

Results.

The flame goes out quickly because the jar has filled with carbon dioxide.

PUTTING CARBON DIOXIDE TO WORK

Procedure (continued):

6. Light another match and again hold it inside the glass. Notice what happens this time.

Results:

The carbon dioxide gas stays in the glass and continues to put out flames for some time after the carbon dioxide gas has stopped bubbling. This is because carbon dioxide is heavier than air.

ACTIVITY 17
Carbon Dioxide Fire Extinguisher #2

For this activity, you will need:
- jar—small but not too short
- vinegar
- candle (shorter than the jar)
- measuring cup
- matches or lighter
- baking soda
- gallon container
- tablespoon
- clay

Procedure:

1. Stick the candle upright in some clay in the bottom of the jar.

2. Light the candle with a match or lighter. Notice what happens to the flame.

Results:

The candle continues to burn. Although the flame is creating carbon dioxide which is heavier than the air in the jar, it doesn't sink because the heat from the flame causes it to rise into the air, so it is continuously replaced with a supply of oxygen from the surrounding air. (Let it continue burning while you do the steps that follow.)

Procedure (continued):

3. Measure out 2 tablespoons of baking soda (66 grams) and pour it into the gallon container.

4. Measure out ½ cup of vinegar and pour it into the container.

PUTTING CARBON DIOXIDE TO WORK

5. As soon as the foaming slows down, carefully pour the gas from the bottle into the jar just as you would pour water. (Make sure you don't pour out the vinegar liquid too.) Notice what happens to the flame.

Results:

The flame goes out as soon as the carbon dioxide gas reaches the candle wick.

Procedure (continued):

You probably still have some fire extinguisher left, so:

6. Quickly re-light the candle. (If the candle doesn't re-light, get rid of leftover carbon dioxide in the jar by pouring it out and try again.)

7. Again, pour the gas from the bottle into the jar to snuff out the flame. (If the gas doesn't put out the flame, add some more vinegar to the gallon container to release more carbon dioxide and try again.)

Results:

You can pour carbon dioxide gas because it is heavier than air. When carbon dioxide gas reaches the flame, it pushes out oxygen and chokes out the flame.

Chapter 17

Acids and Bases

There are many different types of chemical compounds, but two opposite types are especially important to know about and to learn to work with.

These two types of chemical compounds are acids and bases.

We know that an **acid** is a substance that has a sour, sharp or biting taste. Some acids also are harsh chemicals, but many of our foods contain acids. Vinegar, lemon juice and grape juice are good examples of foods that contain acids that can be eaten safely.

Some acids are solids. For example, citric acid is naturally found in oranges, lemons, limes and other tart fruits. You can also buy it in powder form to mix in water. Citric acid water can be used to keep sliced apples or bananas from turning brown.

The opposite of an acid is a **base**, a substance that has a bitter taste, and in water feels slippery. Most bases are harsh laboratory chemicals and are not safe to eat, but you can safely taste a little baking soda or a medicine called Milk of Magnesia, which is a stronger base. In general, most non-food acids and most bases are not safe to taste.

We have been dealing with a household base (baking soda) and a household acid (an ingredient of vinegar). Handled carefully, these two "opposites" are quite safe.

ACIDS AND BASES

ACTIVITY 18
Taste a Safe Acid and a Safe Base

For this activity, you will need:
- vinegar or lemon juice
- Milk of Magnesia or baking soda
- tap water
- 2 cotton swabs
- glass

Procedure:

All items for tasting must be food-grade quality. Utensils must be clean and okay to use with food. Do not use food items or utensils in this activity that may have come into contact with any other chemicals.

1. Pour a bit of vinegar or lemon juice onto the side of a cotton swab. Then taste this liquid containing an acid.

2. Pour a bit of Milk of Magnesia onto another cotton swab or dissolve a little baking soda in about an ounce of water in the glass. Then taste this liquid containing a base.

Chapter 18

A Quick Look at Electricity

We will explore the universe of acids and bases in more detail. But first we need to take a little closer look at what atoms are like and how they can behave.

And to do that, we need to know a bit about electricity.

ELECTRICITY

Electricity is not really a *thing*; it is more just a way that matter is. In other words, it's a characteristic of matter. We know of other basic characteristics of matter. One is that matter has weight and that it takes up space. Electricity is another basic characteristic of matter.

So, what do we mean by "characteristic?" Let's use people for an example.

People have many characteristics such as height and weight. Another obvious one is hair color—people have hair color. We have names for the ways this characteristic shows up in people, like *brown*, *blond*, *grey*, etc. Hair color is just one of the things about people. It is a characteristic of people—people come with these different hair colors.

Like hair color, electricity is just one of the things about matter—a characteristic of matter.

It turns out that the electricity characteristic of matter comes in three different kinds.

These three different kinds have been given the names *positive, negative and neutral*.

A QUICK LOOK AT ELECTRICITY

Positive and *negative* are names that were invented to show the "oppositeness" of those two types of matter. *Neutral* was a good name to show the "in-between-ness" of the third type.

So we could say that matter has the electricity characteristic about the way people have hair color. Matter can be positive, negative or neutral. People can be blond, black-haired, red-headed, etc.

Now we are ready to give a proper definition for electricity:

> **Electricity** is a characteristic of matter. The characteristic is that matter comes in three different kinds, which are called positive, negative and neutral.

We use + to show positive and − to show negative.

The important thing is to know the rules of how these different kinds of matter interact with each other:

- Positive bits of matter repel (push away from) each other.

- Negative bits of matter repel each other.

- A positive bit and a negative bit attract each other.

- Neutral bits don't attract or repel other bits.

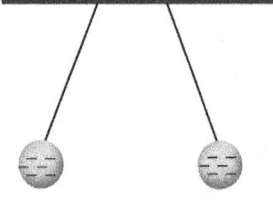
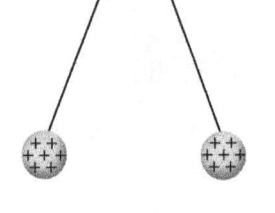
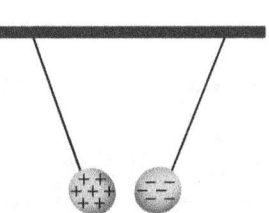
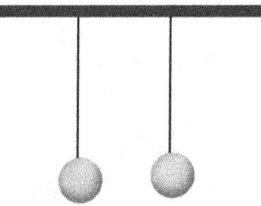

You will learn many things about how the electrical nature of matter shows up in the world. If you keep this understanding of these words, it will make more and more sense.

Chapter 19

Electricity and Atoms

In Chapter 4, we learned about the structure and the parts of an atom—neutrons and protons in the nucleus, and electrons orbiting around it.

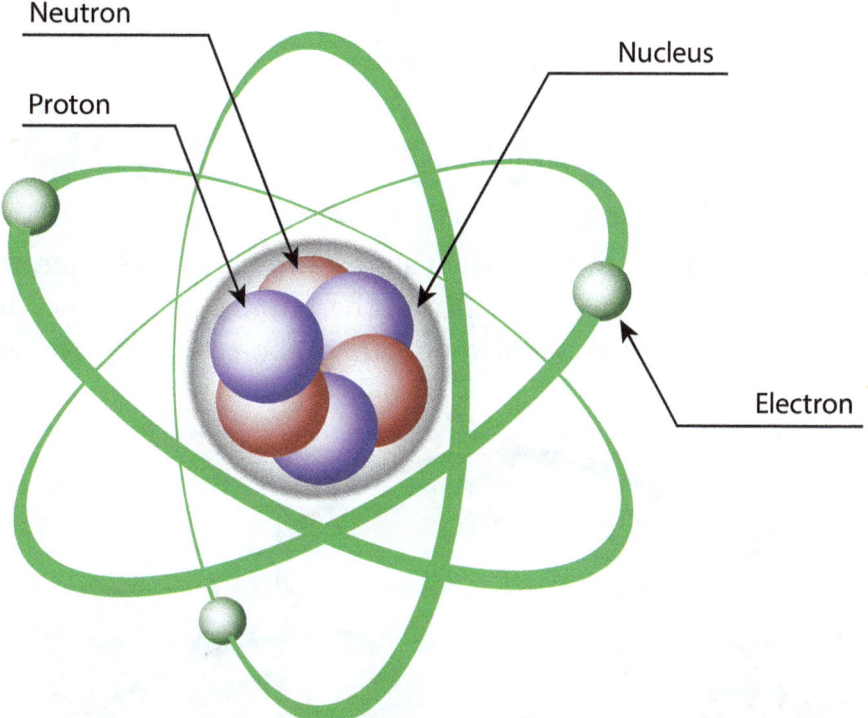

ATOM STRUCTURE

Now you're going to find out what electricity has to do with atoms. And what electricity has to do with how chemical reactions happen.

We know there are three kinds of matter: positive, negative and neutral. An atom contains all three kinds.

ELECTRICITY AND ATOMS

The electrons are the negative kind of matter. Again, this is shown by the symbol -.

The protons are the positive kind of matter. This is shown by the symbol +.

Because the neutrons are neutral, the positive protons make the nucleus the positive kind of matter.

When an atom has the same number of negative electrons as positive protons in the nucleus, they balance each other. This makes the atom itself neutral matter. That's what you can see in this illustration.

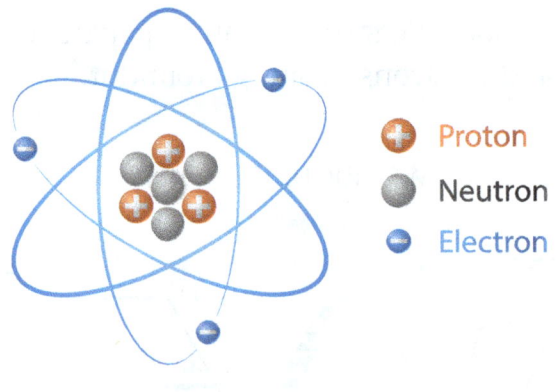

Normally atoms are neutral. However, when atoms and molecules interact, some atoms "like" to grab an extra electron or two from other atoms. And some atoms "like" to give up an electron or two. This can also be true of molecules or groups of atoms.

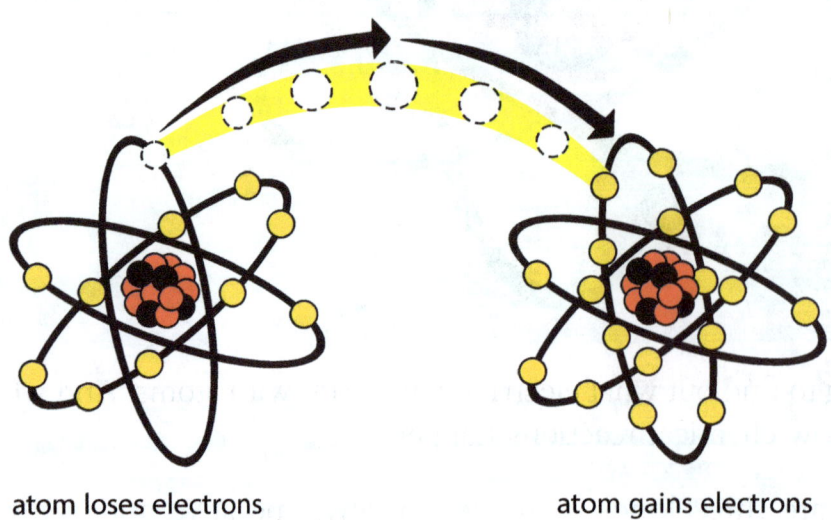

This makes the atoms and molecules no longer neutral—some have "too few" electrons (positive) and some have "too many" (negative).

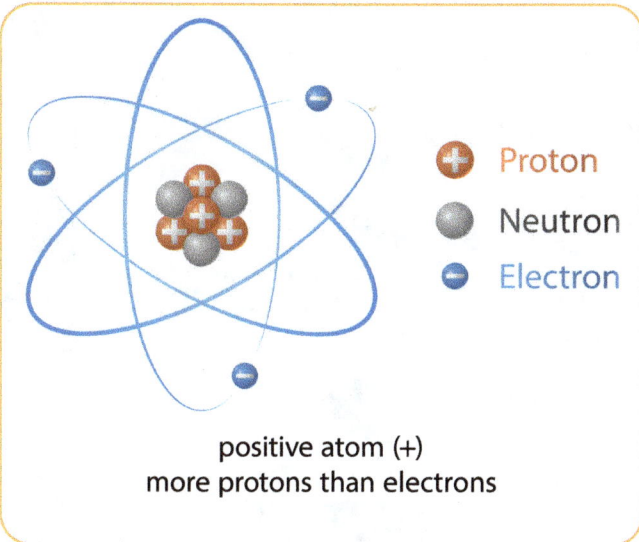

positive atom (+)
more protons than electrons

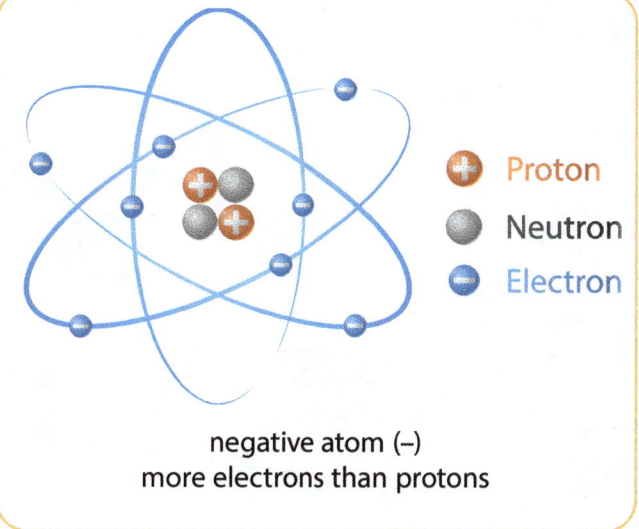

negative atom (−)
more electrons than protons

This is important in chemistry because it can affect how atoms and molecules join up to make new substances.

In other words, this is how chemical reactions happen!

We will not look farther inside the atom, but do remember that electrons can move from atoms to atoms and from molecules to molecules.

Chapter 20

Charged Atoms

When an atom or group of atoms has extra electrons or is missing some, it is no longer neutral. Then we call it **charged**.

Charge is the overall amount of electrical energy in an atom or group of atoms caused by too many electrons (negative) or too few electrons (positive).

(If you are interested in learning a bit more about this, you can read "More about Electrical Charge" in the appendix.)

IONS

Once an atom becomes charged, we no longer call it an atom. A charged atom or group of atoms gets a new name: **ions**.

If an atom has one or more extra electrons, it is called a **negative ion**.

If it has lost one or more electrons, it is called a **positive ion**.

Why is this important? When atoms are charged, that affects how they interact.

Opposite charges attract each other and similar charges repel each other. So a negative ion can be attracted toward a positive ion and repelled by other negative ions.

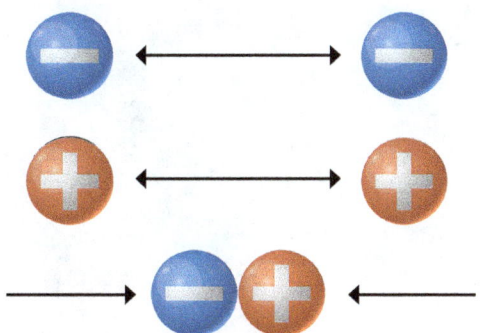

CHARGED ATOMS

This can make a difference when atoms are coming together to form molecules during reactions.

In the next chapter, we will learn how this relates to acids and bases.

Chapter 21
What Makes Acids and Bases Opposite?

We know that acids and bases are opposites, and that when they are combined, there is a reaction.

But why is this? What makes them opposites? Why do they react?

This is a fundamental of chemistry that applies all the way from baking soda and vinegar volcanoes to how you clean your home or digest your food. It is worth knowing about.

When studying acids and bases, there are two particular ions we always see.

One is a hydrogen atom that has lost an electron and has become positive. Its symbol is **H$^+$**. Acids have positive H$^+$ ions.

The other is a hydrogen-oxygen group that has gained an extra electron and has become negative. Its symbol is **OH$^-$**. Bases have negative OH$^-$ ions.

So what do we mean when we say acids and bases are "opposite"?

WHAT MAKES ACIDS AND BASES OPPOSITE?

ACIDS HAVE POSITIVE H+ IONS

What makes acids different from other chemicals is that each acid molecule contains one or more hydrogen atoms (**H**) that are loosely held onto by the molecule.

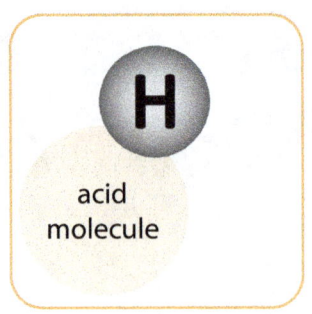

an acid molecule with a loosely held hydrogen atom.

When the acid is dissolved in water, these loose **H**'s tend to drift away from the rest of the acid molecule.

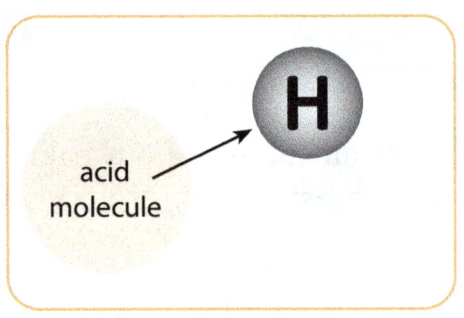

In liquid form, the hydrogen can separate.

When the hydrogens come loose like that, they leave an electron behind with the rest of the molecule. The hydrogens become positive (**H+**) ions floating around. These hydrogen ions are free to react with other atoms or molecules. We say that this solution becomes **acidic**, which just means it has some of these loose positive hydrogen ions floating around.

Because the hydrogens leave an electron behind in the rest of the molecule, that remaining part now has an extra electron, making it into a negative ion, and we can improve the last illustration like this:

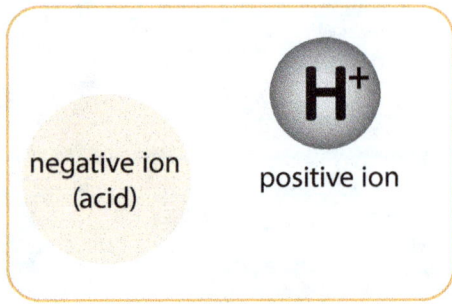

When the loose hydrogen separates, it leaves an electron behind. The hydrogen becomes a positive ion and the remaining part becomes a negative ion.

So the big thing about acids is that they have these loose positive hydrogen ions ready to react if they can find something to react with.

We have done several activities with the acid in vinegar (acetic acid), which has been safe to work with because it is not too strong of an acid *and* it is diluted in water. Its important contribution in our activities has been that it does what all acids do—releases positive hydrogen ions into the solution.

BASES HAVE NEGATIVE OH⁻ IONS

Something similar but opposite happens with bases. What makes bases different is that each molecule of the base has one (or more) hydrogen-oxygen (**OH**) group that are part of the molecule, but the *group* is not held tightly to the rest of the molecule. The **OH** group is called a "hydroxide group."

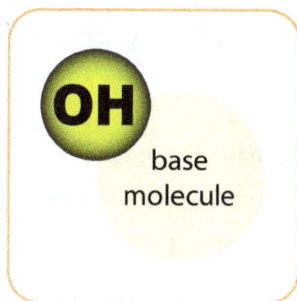

a base molecule with a loosely held hydroxide group.

When the base is in a water solution, these **OH**'s tend to drift free of the rest of the molecule.

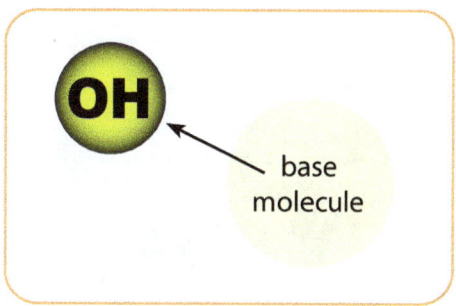

In liquid form, the hydroxide group can separate.

When the hydroxide group comes loose like that, it takes an extra electron from the rest of the molecule and it becomes an **OH⁻** ion floating around. These negative hydroxide ions are free to react with other atoms or molecules. We say that this solution becomes **basic**, which just means it has some of these loose negative hydroxide ions floating around ready to react.

WHAT MAKES ACIDS AND BASES OPPOSITE?

Opposite to the story with acids, where an electron is left behind, the hydroxide group has "stolen" an electron from the rest of the base molecule. So the remaining part now has too few electrons, making it into a positive ion. And we can again improve the last illustration like this:

When the loose hydroxide group separates, it takes an extra electron with it. It becomes a negative ion and the remaining part becomes a positive ion.

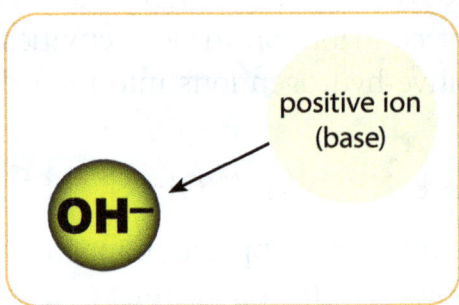

Similar but opposite to what we saw with acids, the big thing about bases is that they have these negative hydroxide ions floating around ready to react if they can find something to react with. A few strong bases will also tend to "eat" into other substances.

We have also worked with the base baking soda, which is safe to work with because it is not too strong. Its important contribution to our activities has been to do what all bases do—release negative hydroxide ions into the solution.

Chapter 22

The Reaction When Acid Meets Base

THE FIRST HALF OF THE REACTION

When an acid and a base are both dissolved in water together, you will have some ions that will "want" to get together because the hydrogen ions are positive and the hydroxide ions are negative. Remember that negatives and positives attract each other.

Imagine we have both the acid and the base in a solution. First we will look just at what happens with the hydrogen ion **H+** and the hydroxide ion **OH−**. (We will see later that this is one-half of the reaction.)

From what we have already learned, it is probably pretty obvious what is going to happen:

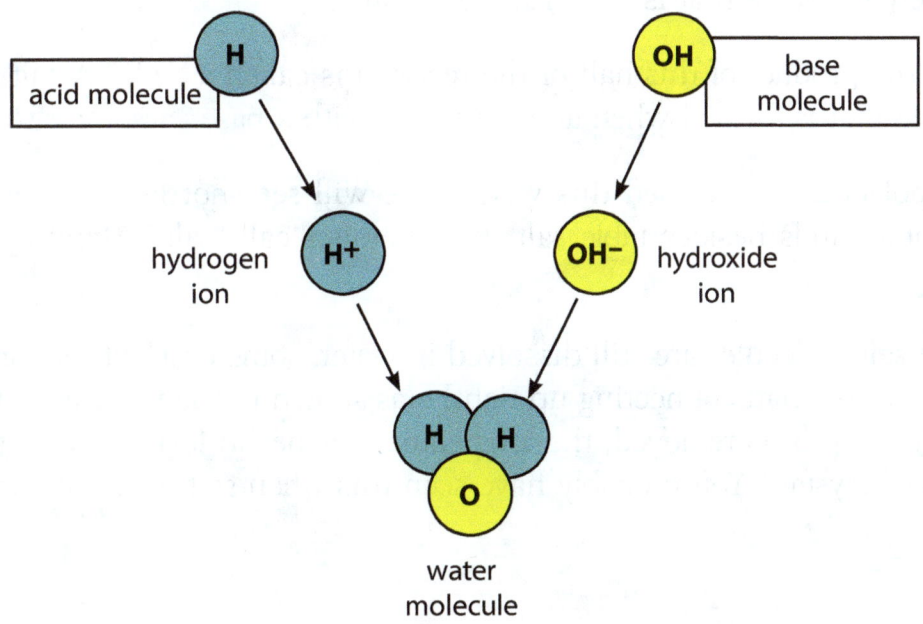

THE REACTION WHEN ACID MEETS BASE

In this half of the chemical reaction, the hydrogen ions and the hydroxide ions react to give water as the product.

The hydroxide group has given its extra electron to the hydrogen ion, so the new water molecule is neutral.

THE SECOND HALF OF THE REACTION

The rest of the acid molecule (now a negative ion) and the rest of the base molecule (now a positive ion) also have opposite charges and they attract each other and join to form a new molecule.

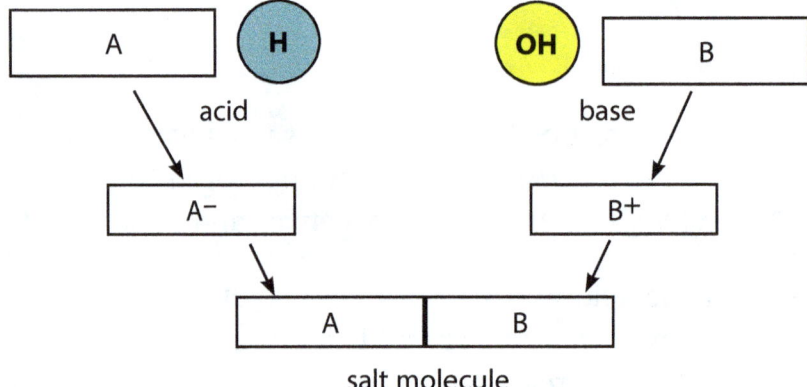

Here the **A−** has "given" its extra electron(s) to the **B+** ion and they have come together to form a new molecule that is electrically neutral.

Notice that the product of this half of the reaction is called a "salt." A salt is the kind of a molecule that is formed when an acid reacts with a base.

Table salt molecules are formed this way, as we will see shortly, but there are other chemical compounds besides table salt that chemists call "salt." Many of these salts are poisons.

When these salt molecules are still dissolved in water, some or all of the ions continue to float free, rather than connecting up tightly (as shown in the illustration). But when the water dries up or is removed, the ions come together to form solid salt molecules in the form of crystals. You probably have seen this when salt water dries up.

THE REACTION WHEN ACID MEETS BASE

BOTH HALVES OF THE REACTION TOGETHER

The overall reaction when an acid and a base react together, including the half of the reaction that produces water and the half of the reaction that produces a salt, is called a **neutralization reaction**. The water produced is neutral—it is neither an acid nor a base. The salt is usually neutral too.

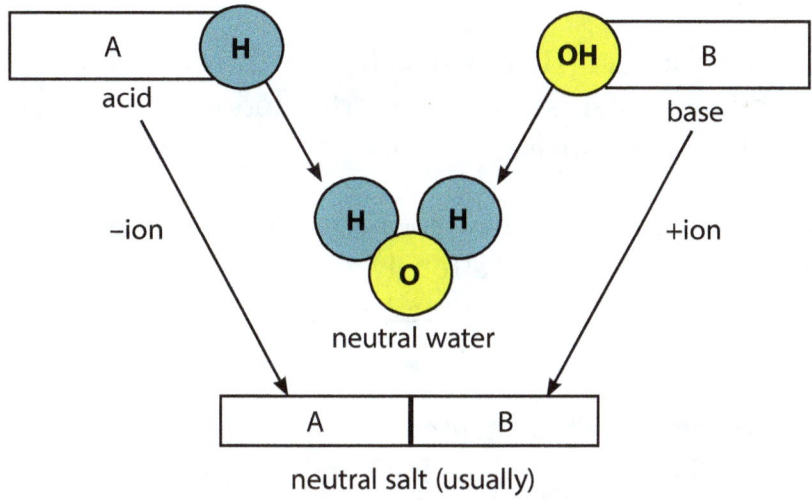

In neutralization, the hydrogen ion from an acid combines with the hydroxide ion of a base to form a neutral water molecule. The other parts of the acid (the – ion) and base (the + ion) combine to form a neutral salt molecule.

You might expect that the reaction we have been working with so often—vinegar and baking soda—is a simple neutralization reaction just like these illustrations. That is not quite the case.

The **H+** and the **OH−** do get together to form water, as you would expect, but the rest of the molecules go through a more complicated reaction.

Actual neutralization reactions tend to be a bit too complicated to do in beginning chemistry. The next section discusses a very simple, but very energetic example.

THE REACTION WHEN ACID MEETS BASE

A DRAMATIC EXAMPLE OF A NEUTRALIZATION REACTION

It was mentioned above that table salt is produced in a neutralization reaction. Salt may seem pretty boring, but this reaction is definitely not.

Here is a neutralization experiment which you will never do—because it is just too dangerous.

It starts with hydrochloric acid (**HCl**) and sodium hydroxide (**NaOH**). When these are concentrated (not diluted) **HCl** is a very powerful and dangerous acid, and **NaOH** is a very powerful and dangerous base.

The reason they are dangerous is they both strongly "want" to react. In fact, if you put them together, they do react very strongly and give off a lot of heat in the process. So much heat that it will produce an explosion! So we will just do an imaginary experiment.

From what we have covered about neutralization, you would expect that a reaction between **HCl** and **NaOH** would produce **H₂O** and table salt **NaCl**, right?

So what is the big deal with just water and salt?

It is the amount of *heat* given off.

Here is an imaginary experimental set-up. Start by imagining a *very* strong glass globe that is sealed but has some way of letting us inject chemicals into it.

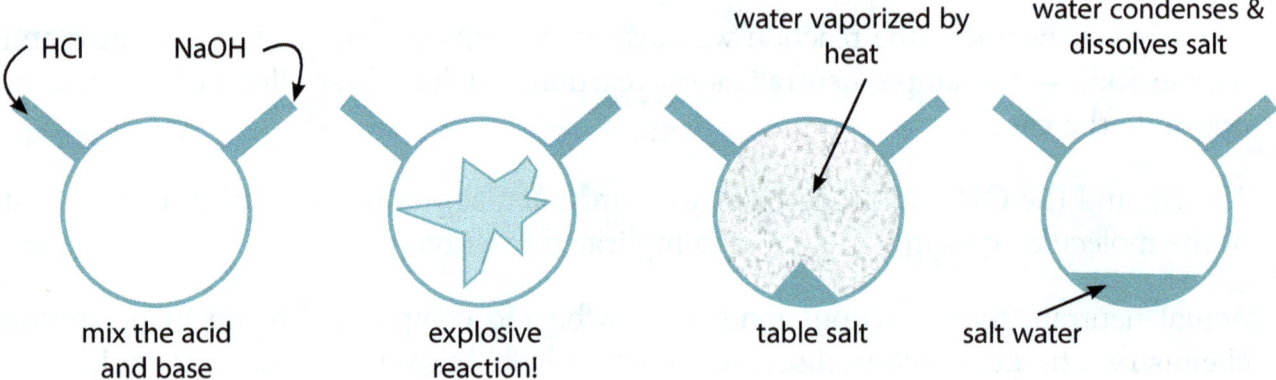

THE REACTION WHEN ACID MEETS BASE

Here is this specific neutralization reaction, yielding salt and water:

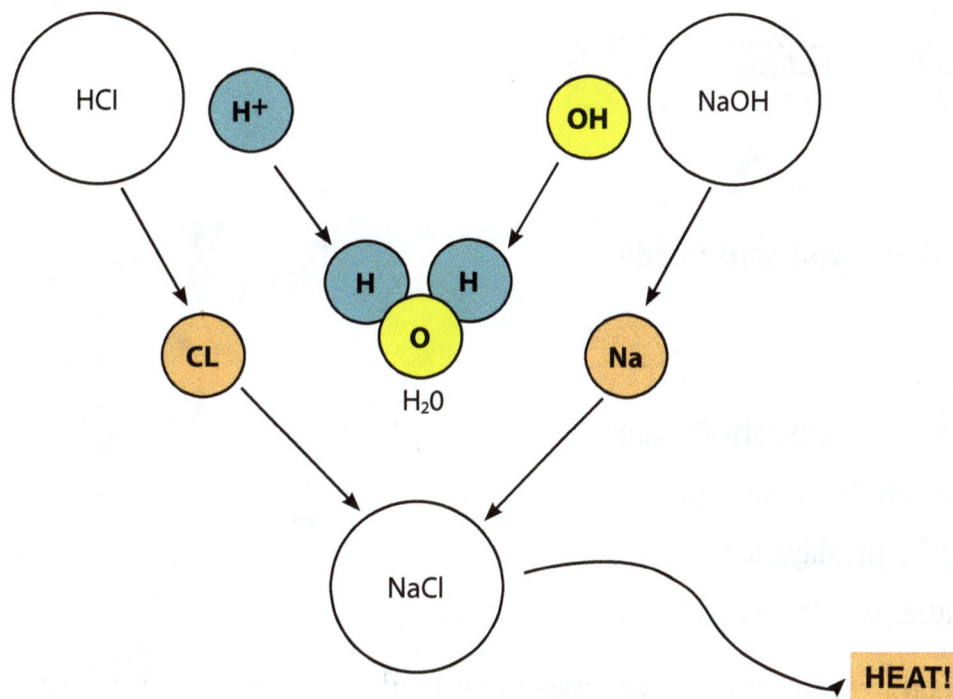

You can see why the container had to be strong. You can use your imagination about what would happen if the container were not strong enough. Fatal accidents have happened from just this particular reaction.

Another simpler way to show what happens is to use a reaction diagram. Compare it to the above illustration.

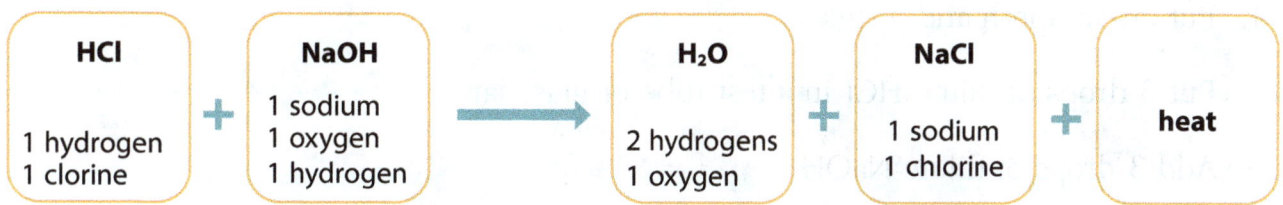

(As is proper with reaction diagrams, the numbers of each kind of atom agree on both sides.)

As a further note about neutralization reactions, they generally produce *some* heat and you can learn more in advanced chemistry about why that is. This reaction is a somewhat extreme case, where a *lot* of heat is generated.

THE REACTION WHEN ACID MEETS BASE

ACTIVITY 19
Neutralization Reaction

For this activity, you will need:
- apron
- goggles
- dilute HCl, or washing soda
- dilute NaOH, or vinegar
- test tube or glass jar
- propane gas burner

If you are using washing soda and vinegar, you will also need water, measuring spoons and a measuring cup

Information:

It is possible to carry out the neutralization reaction discussed in Chapter 22 safely by using a *diluted* form of HCl and NaOH. This can be done using the actual diluted chemicals or by using washing soda and vinegar.

Procedure (if you have dilute HCl and NaOH):

1. Put on an apron and goggles.

2. Put 3 drops of dilute HCl in a test tube or glass jar.

3. Add 3 drops of dilute NaOH.

4. Heat the mixture over a propane flame until all the water evaporates.

Procedure (if you have washing soda and vinegar):

1. Put on an apron and goggles.

2. Mix 1/4 tsp. washing soda in 1/4 cup of water.

3. Put 5 drops of the liquid in a test tube or glass jar.

4. Add 4 drops of vinegar to a test tube or glass jar. (The mixture will bubble and give off carbon dioxide gas.)

5. Wait a minute for the bubbling to slow down. Then heat the mixture over a gas burner or flame until all the water evaporates.

Results:

A white powder will form at the bottom of the test tube/jar. This white powder is NaCl formed from the neutralization of HCl and NaOH.

In other words, it is a salt formed by the neutralization of an acid and a base.

Chapter 23

A Scale of the Strengths of Acids and Bases

The scale on the next page lists some common chemicals and foods, and shows how acidic or basic they are compared to neutral distilled water. (**Distilled water** is water that has been boiled into vapor and condensed back into water. This removes impurities.)

Remember that acidic means that, in solution, there are loose positive hydrogen ions floating around, and basic means there are loose negative hydroxide groups floating around.

At the top end of the scale are the most acidic compounds. That means they have the most loose hydrogens and practically no loose hydroxides.

The compounds at the bottom of the scale are the most basic ones. They have the most loose hydroxides and practically no loose hydrogens.

In the neutral middle band there are few loose hydrogens and hydroxides.

On the acidic end of the scale there are many foods that you eat.

On the basic end are many chemicals that are used for cleaning and washing, and not so many that are safe to eat.

A SCALE OF THE STRENGTHS OF ACIDS AND BASES

EXTREMELY ACIDIC — battery acid, stomach acid

STRONGLY ACIDIC — lemon, grapefruit and orange juices; cola soft drinks, vinegar; apple and grape juices

MODERATELY ACIDIC — tomato juice, yogurt

WEAKLY ACIDIC — rainwater, coffee; many vegetables; fresh milk

NEUTRAL — clear water, especially freshly distilled water

WEAKLY BASIC — saliva, blood; raw eggs; seawater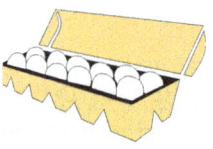

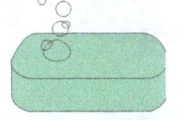

MODERATELY BASIC — hand soap, toothpaste; baking soda dissolved in water

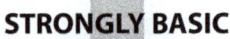

STRONGLY BASIC — Milk of Magnesia, ammonia cleaner

EXTREMELY BASIC — lime (a white compound of calcium and oxygen); household chlorine bleach; oven cleaner

98

A SCALE OF THE STRENGTHS OF ACIDS AND BASES

SHOWING ACIDS AND BASES WITH A COLOR CHANGE

Chemists have several ways to test to see whether something is acidic, or basic, or neutral.

One way is to use a special test substance that turns one color when it is added to a base and turns another color when it is added to an acid.

A substance that does this is called an **indicator**. For example, red cabbage has a **pigment** (a chemical that shows color) in it that works as an indicator and is simple to use.

We will make cabbage juice indicator in the next activity. (Ready-made commercial cabbage juice indicators can also be purchased—Red Cabbage Jiffy Juice powder is one brand that is often used.)

When a ready-made indicator, or your own red cabbage juice indicator, is mixed in water, it is normally a violet color. It will change colors in the presence of other substances, such as vinegar and baking soda, depending on whether they are acidic or basic.

Here is what the colors mean:

red	acidic
purple to violet	moderately acidic
violet*	neutral
blue	moderately basic
green	strongly basic

*Water may be a bit acidic or basic so the color of the cabbage juice may vary. A pinch of baking soda will turn purple to violet and a drop or two of vinegar will turn blue to violet.

A SCALE OF THE STRENGTHS OF ACIDS AND BASES

ACTIVITY 20
Make a Red Cabbage Indicator

For this activity, you will need:
- red cabbage
- white vinegar
- measuring cup
- baking soda
- hot plate, or microwave oven
- water
- pan or microwavable container
- eye dropper

Procedure:

1. Chop up (medium fine) enough red cabbage to fill half a cup (or more if you want to have plenty—it can be used for many activities).

Do #2 *or* #3. Then continue at #4:

2. Using a hot plate: Place the cabbage pieces in a pan and add an equal amount of water. Heat until the water boils and turns dark.

3. Using a microwave oven: Place the cabbage pieces and water in equal amounts in a microwaveable container. Microwave until the water boils and turns dark.

4. When the container cools enough, hold your hand over the top of the container to keep the cabbage pieces in and pour the liquid into a glass. Remove any cabbage pieces and throw them in the trash. The colored liquid is your cabbage juice indicator.

5. The cabbage juice may be blue or blue-green, or even green at this point, but it needs to be violet to blue (neutral) for the activities you are going to do. If it is on the green side of neutral according to the table on page 99, add vinegar drop by drop (and swirl or stir) until the liquid is a neutral color according to the table. If the color is toward the red side of neutral, add pinches of baking soda until you get it to neutral.)

You will be using your indicator in the next activity. If you won't be doing it right away, store your indicator in the refrigerator.

A SCALE OF THE STRENGTHS OF ACIDS AND BASES

ACTIVITY 21
Using an Acid-Base Indicator

For this activity, you will need:

- cabbage juice indicator (commercial, such as Red Cabbage Jiffy Juice, or homemade)
- white vinegar
- eye dropper
- 2 clear glasses or jars
- baking soda
- white sheet of paper
- household ammonia cleaner
- tablespoon
- distilled water
- spoon (for stirring)

Procedure:

1. Add 2 tablespoons of the indicator solution to a glass or jar.

2. Place the glass with the indicator in it on top of a white sheet of paper so that you can see the color clearly.

3. The indicator juice needs to start out violet (neutral) for the activities you are going to do. If the indicator juice isn't in that range, first do the actions in step 5 of the previous activity to bring it into that range.

4. Mix a small amount of water with the indicator in the glass. Does the indicator change color?

Results:

The indicator should not change color much. Tap water usually is very close to neutral. If this is not true, try using distilled water where water is needed below.

Procedure (continued):

5. Continue to add vinegar drop by drop to the glass (and swirl or stir) until the liquid turns to a purple or red color. This is a lighter color than red cabbage.

Results:

The color indicates that the liquid is now acidic.

Procedure (continued):

6. Add baking soda to the glass, a pinch at a time, and swirl or stir until the liquid turns to a neutral color again.

7. Add baking soda, a pinch at a time, and swirl or stir until the liquid turns blue or blue-green.

Results:

The color indicates that the liquid is now moderately basic.

Procedure (continued):

8. Add household ammonia cleaner a drop at a time (and swirl or stir) until the liquid turns green.

Results:

The color indicates that the liquid has become strongly basic. Even though the pigment gets more dilute as you add more liquid, the pigment from the red cabbage shows whether the liquid is acidic, basic or neutral.

Procedure (continued):

9. Discard the indicator and rinse the glass.

A SCALE OF THE STRENGTHS OF ACIDS AND BASES

ACTIVITY 22
Test for Acids and Bases with Cabbage Juice Indicator

For this activity, you will need:

- cabbage juice indicator (commercial, such as Red Cabbage Jiffy Juice, or homemade)
- sheet of paper for making a chart
- 2 clear glasses or jars
- white sheet of paper
- tablespoon
- Various substances to test such as: lemon, grapefruit or orange juice, plain yogurt, hydrogen peroxide, soil in water, milk, distilled water, powdered antacid, liquid soap, toothpaste, egg white, Milk of Magnesia, oven cleaner, toilet bowl cleaner

Information:

In this activity, you will be picking various substances and testing them. The substances you pick must be able to dissolve in water for the indicator to work. It doesn't work with oily substances.

A. Collect at least five substances to test.

B. Make a table on a sheet of paper like the one below so that you can write down each substance you test and the results. Refer back to the color chart on page 99 as needed. (One example is filled out for you below.)

Item	Color of Indicator	Acid or Base
grapefruit juice	magenta	acidic

A SCALE OF THE STRENGTHS OF ACIDS AND BASES

Procedure:

For each substance you test, do this:

1. Put 1 tablespoon of cabbage juice indicator in the glass (or jar).

2. Place the glass on white paper so you can see the color easily.

3. Add a tablespoon of tap water.

4. Add some of the substance you are testing. An amount equal to a tablespoon should do. (Milk uses only a drop.)

5. Using the table you made, write down the results.

6. Continue testing the substances until you have tested at least five. Rinse out the glass and add new cabbage indicator for each test.

Sample of Results:

Actual results may vary somewhat.

item	color of indicator	acid or base
lemon, grapefruit or orange juice	purple-violet	moderately acidic
plain yogurt	purple-violet	moderately acidic
hydrogen peroxide	violet	acidic to neutral (Some commercial products have additives that change how acidic it is.)
soil in water	purple to violet but variable	variable, but likely acidic (some desert soils are basic)
milk (use only a drop)	violet or a bit redder	neutral or slightly acidic
distilled water	violet to purple	acidic to neutral. (If tap water is left standing for long, it usually picks up carbon dioxide from the air and becomes slightly acidic.)
powdered antacid	blue to blue-green	neutral to weakly basic

A SCALE OF THE STRENGTHS OF ACIDS AND BASES

item	color of indicator	acid or base
liquid soap	blue to blue-green	moderately basic (variable)
toothpaste	blue to blue-green	moderately basic
egg white	blue-green to green	moderately to strongly basic
Milk of Magnesia	green	strongly basic
oven cleaner	green	strongly basic
toilet bowl cleaner or other spray cleaner	green or purple	strongly basic or acidic (different cleaners are made from different chemicals)

ACTIVITY 23A
Ammonia Cleaner, Epsom Salt and Vinegar

For this activity, you will need:

- cabbage juice indicator (commercial, such as Red Cabbage Jiffy Juice, or homemade)
- measuring spoons
- Epsom salt
- household ammonia cleaner
- microwave
- white vinegar
- white sheet of paper
- tap water
- notebook paper to record results
- glass or jar

Information:

Any acid can neutralize any base if you add the chemicals together in the right amounts. As you have seen, if you add an indicator to the mix, it will change color at each step in response to changes in acidity.

The next activities feature chemical reactions that cause the chemicals to rearrange so that one of the chemicals forms a solid that settles out of the solution and another is dissolved in the solution. By adding an indicator, you can see the changes in acidity that take place during the chemical reactions at each step.

When ammonia is dissolved in water, it forms a base called ammonium hydroxide, which is sometimes used as a household cleaner.

A SCALE OF THE STRENGTHS OF ACIDS AND BASES

If you mix household ammonia cleaner with Epsom salt (magnesium sulfate), a white solid forms. If you then add enough vinegar acid, the white solid disappears. With each change, the acidity of the solution also changes.

Procedure:

Part 1.

Note the results as you go:

1. Starting with an empty glass (or jar), add 2 tablespoons of cabbage juice indicator.

2. Add 2 tablespoons of tap water.

3. Place the glass on a white sheet of paper so that you can see the color clearly. What color is the liquid?

Results:

Violet. The liquid should still be neutral.

Procedure (continued):

4. Add a 1/2 teaspoon of Epsom salt and stir until it dissolves. What color is the liquid now?

Results:

Still in the neutral range. The Epsom salt does not change the acidity.

Procedure (continued):

5. Add 4 tablespoons of ammonia cleaner. What color is the liquid now?

Results:

The liquid turns a milky green and is strongly basic from adding ammonia.

The color indicates the solution is very basic.

A SCALE OF THE STRENGTHS OF ACIDS AND BASES

Procedure:

Part 2.

The second part of the activity is to neutralize this base solution with vinegar acid.

1. Add vinegar one tablespoon at a time and stir until the solution becomes clear. What color is the liquid now?

Results:

The solution is neutralized by acid in the vinegar and the liquid becomes clear again, but the liquid is still green and strongly basic. This takes about 2 tablespoons of vinegar.

Procedure (continued):

2. Continue stirring in vinegar one tablespoon at a time until the liquid shows the neutral color. How many tablespoons of vinegar does that take?

Results:

It should take about 2 more tablespoons of vinegar.

Procedure (continued):

3. Continue stirring in vinegar one tablespoon at a time until the liquid is acidic. What is the color? How many tablespoons of vinegar does that take?

Results:

The color is on the red side of violet. It should take about 1 more tablespoon of vinegar.

A SCALE OF THE STRENGTHS OF ACIDS AND BASES

ACTIVITY 23B
Washing Soda, Epsom Salt and Lemon Juice

For this activity, you will need:

- cabbage juice indicator (commercial, such as Red Cabbage Jiffy Juice, or homemade)
- 2 small glasses/jars
- Epsom salt (magnesium sulfate)
- measuring spoons
- washing soda (sodium carbonate)
- lemon juice (reconstituted is okay)
- white paper
- water
- notebook paper to record results
- microwave oven or hot plate
- spoon (for stirring)

Procedure:

Part 1.

1. Add 5 tablespoons of cabbage juice indicator to each of 2 small glasses. Make sure the color is in the neutral range, and if not, adjust it as you have done before.

2. Measure out 1/2 teaspoon (6.3 grams) of washing soda (sodium carbonate) and add it to the first glass.

3. Place the glass on a white sheet of paper so that you can see the color clearly. What color is the liquid now?

A SCALE OF THE STRENGTHS OF ACIDS AND BASES

Results:

The liquid is strongly basic from the sodium carbonate and turns green.

Procedure (continued):

4. Place the second glass on a white sheet of paper so that you can see the color clearly.

5. Measure out 1/2 teaspoon (6.7 grams) of Epsom salt (magnesium sulfate) and add it to the second glass. What color is the liquid now?

Results:

Still in the neutral range. The Epsom salt does not change the acidity.

Procedure (continued):

6. Heat both glasses and stir until the chemicals dissolve. (In a microwave oven, it should take about 45 seconds.)

7. Stir both glasses until the chemicals dissolve.

8. Pour the contents of one glass into the other and watch what happens.

Results:

The solution immediately turns milky green as a white solid forms and begins to settle out.

A reaction occurs where parts of the two compounds trade places. The white solid is magnesium carbonate, which reacts with water and forms a base, while the compound sodium sulfate remains dissolved in the solution.

sodium carbonate + magnesium sulfate
turns to
magnesium carbonate and sodium sulfate

The color indicates the solution is still very basic.

A SCALE OF THE STRENGTHS OF ACIDS AND BASES

Procedure:

Part 2.

The second part of the activity is to neutralize magnesium carbonate with lemon juice. Lemon juice contains citric acid, which is stronger than vinegar acid.

1. Add lemon juice one teaspoon at a time, stirring each time, until the white magnesium carbonate begins to dissolve. What color is the liquid now?

Results:

Some of the magnesium carbonate is partially neutralized by the acid in the lemon juice and the liquid begins to clear up, but still is green and very basic. This should take about 4 teaspoons of lemon juice.

Procedure (continued):

2. Continue stirring in lemon juice one teaspoon at a time until the liquid begins to turn blue and most of the magnesium carbonate is dissolved.

Results:

The color change indicates the solution is now weakly basic. This should take about 3 more teaspoons of lemon juice.

Procedure (continued):

3. Continue stirring in lemon juice one teaspoon at a time until you achieve a neutral color. How many more teaspoons of lemon juice does this take?

Results:

The color may be weak because the solution has been diluted so much. It should take about 3 more teaspoons of lemon juice.

Chapter 24

Crystals

In some solid compounds, the molecules can line up in a regular pattern. You could say these molecules "like" to fit together in a certain repeating way. When this happens, the substance appears in regular shapes with flat surfaces. These are called **crystals**. Crystals may be made up of individual atoms or of molecules.

Table salt and sugar can form crystals, and snowflakes are crystals of the solid form of water (ice). Even metals can form crystals. Most solid substances that aren't mixtures of things can form crystals if conditions are right.

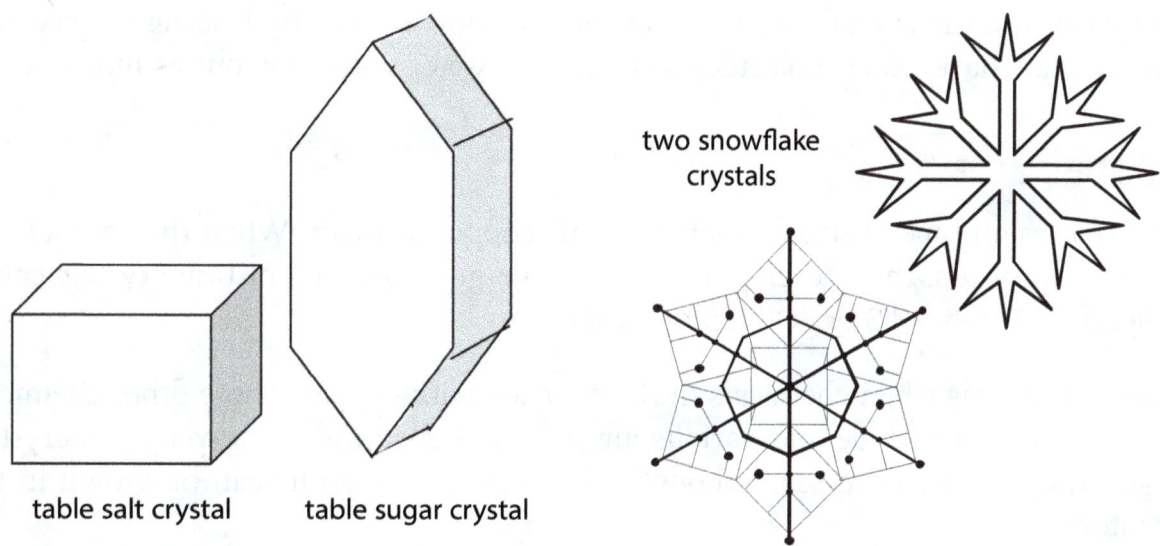

table salt crystal   table sugar crystal   two snowflake crystals

Crystals come in many shapes, sizes and colors. Sometimes a chemical can be identified by its crystals alone.

113

CRYSTALS

GROWING CRYSTALS

When you stir sugar into liquids like water, milk or juice, the sugar grains get smaller and soon disappear. The molecules of sugar are still there, but now they are spread throughout the liquid.

As discussed earlier, liquid with chemicals dissolved in it is called a solution or a chemical solution. If your sugar solution is thick enough, it also is called a *syrup*.

You can separate out solid sugar from syrup (solution) and make crystals. First, dissolve as much sugar as you can in hot water. Then let the liquid cool slowly. If the liquid cools fast, the sugar will form solid grains with no specific shape, but if the liquid cools slowly, sugar crystals will form over several days. The longer you leave the liquid alone, the larger the crystals can grow.

SOME CRYSTALS HOLD WATER

Crystals usually seem quite dry, but some types of crystals actually have water molecules tied up inside them and are known as **hydrated crystals**.

Whether or not the crystals are hydrated can be shown easily by heating the crystals. If the crystals have water molecules in them, the water will come out as moisture.

COLORFUL CRYSTALS OF COPPER

Many statues and metal structures have some copper in them. When they are left out in the air for years, they develop a green to blue-green coating of tiny crystals called verdigris (VER-deh-GRIS or –GREES or -GREE).

Verdigris happens when chemicals in the air react with copper. These other chemicals are water, carbon dioxide and various air pollution chemicals. The verdigris crystals are generally too small to see, although larger verdigris crystals can be grown in the laboratory.

The color of the copper compounds depends on several things. If there is only a little water present in the crystals, the color could be light green. If there is more water in the crystals, the color could be blue-green, and if there is a lot of water in the crystals, the color could be bluer still. All of these variations are called verdigris.

Some other copper compounds have specific colors. Copper forms a blue compound with ammonia and a green compound with acetic acid in vinegar. Copper can form black compounds with oxygen and sulfur (sometimes there is sulfur in air pollution). The turquoise stone that is popular in jewelry contains a copper compound that gives it its color.

CRYSTALS

ACTIVITY 24
Grow Crystals of Sugar: Finish

For this activity, you will need:
- magnifying glass
- tap water
- dishwashing liquid
- cloth or sponge

Information:

This is a continuation of Activity 4 Grow Crystals of Sugar: Start.

Procedure:

1. Get your glass and waxed paper that you prepared in Activity 4, and look at your crystals with the magnifying glass in bright light.

Results:

When you first checked your growing crystals: On the wax paper, the sugar appears as glassy or frosty material after the water evaporates. Because it happened quickly, you may or may not be able to spot crystals with the magnifying glass.

Now: The stick will be coated with clear sugar crystals which have very definite shapes. If you compare (with a magnifying glass) the sugar grains you started with and sugar crystals you made, you may see quite a difference. The starting grains were probably mostly made by crushing crystals.

Note: If you prepared the sugar crystals in a kitchen equipped for cooking, you can eat the crystals when you are finished. However, if you used lab materials, *do not* eat them because the lab equipment has probably been used with unsafe chemicals.

Special Cleanup:

After you have finished the activity, rinse the syrup out of the glass with lots of warm water. If it is too thick to rinse out, add hot water and try again after it has softened up some. You could also microwave it. You may want to add a little dishwashing liquid as well.

CRYSTALS

ACTIVITY 25
Grow Salt Crystals

For this activity, you will need:
- glass or jar—large, clear, heat-proof
- measuring cup
- magnifying glass
- tap water
- tape
- clean slender stick
- waxed paper
- salt
- tablespoon
- cloth or sponge

Information:

If you like, you can also grow crystals of salt by following many of the same steps for growing sugar crystals, but it doesn't take as long.

You can't dissolve as much salt in water as you can sugar, so instead of using 3/4 cup of sugar, dissolve just 2 tablespoons of salt in a half cup of hot water. The crystals will turn out to be a different shape, and salt is easier to clean up than sugar. If you put a teaspoonful of the salt solution on a piece of wax paper, it will dry to a white flakey material that contains some tiny crystals.

Procedure:

1. Look at some grains of salt with a magnifying glass. See if the grains tend to have a regular shape with some flat faces or not. Some crystals may have been crushed, but some may be intact.

2. Wet an inch or two of one end of the stick and roll it in salt so that it is somewhat coated with salt. Set it aside to dry for about 20 minutes.

3. Dissolve 2 tablespoons of salt in a half cup of very hot water. Stir it until it is fully dissolved.

4. Take out a teaspoonful of the salt solution and pour it on a piece of waxed paper. Set it aside.

5. Use tape to position the stick more or less vertically in the container with the coated end in the salt solution. The stick can rest on the bottom.

6. Set the glass and wax paper away in a warm place where they will be undisturbed while they grow. Check them from time to time and look at them with the magnifying glass in bright light. You should start to see crystals in a few days.

Results:

When you first check your growing crystals: On the wax paper, the salt appears as a white, frosty material after the water evaporates. Because it happened quickly, you may or may not be able to spot crystals with the magnifying glass.

Later: The stick and possibly the glass will be coated with salt crystals which may have very definite shapes. If you compare (using a magnifying glass) the salt grains you started with and salt crystals you made, you may see quite a difference. The starting grains were probably mostly made by crushing crystals.

CRYSTALS

ACTIVITY 26
Grow Epsom Salt Crystals on Glass

For this activity, you will need:
- Epsom salt (magnesium sulfate)
- microwave and microwave safe container, or hot plate and pan
- teaspoon
- measuring cup
- glass or jar
- flat glass plate
- tap water
- cotton wad
- magnifying glass

Procedure:

1. Heat ¼ cup of water in the container/pan to near boiling.

2. Add 2 tablespoons of Epsom salt. Heat and stir until it's all dissolved (about 1 minute in a microwave).

3. Spread out some of the mixture on a glass or glass-like surface with a cotton wad. Try to spread it evenly.

4. If possible, turn on a fan to speed up evaporation. Crystals will begin to form. Once the growth stops, look at the crystals with the magnifying glass.

Results:

In about 10 minutes the magnesium sulfate crystallizes out on the glass surface. It forms needle-like crystals in all directions until the whole surface is covered with a frost-like pattern of crystals.

Special Cleanup:

When you are finished, wash the pan and glass plate thoroughly so that all the magnesium sulfate crystals dissolve and wash away.

ACTIVITY 27
Get Water Out of Crystals

For this activity, you will need:
- gas burner, or pan and hot plate
- Epsom salt
- 2 test tubes and test tube holder or 2 glasses/jars
- table salt
- teaspoon
- magnifying glass
- matches or lighter

Information:

In this activity you will compare table salt and Epsom salt to see which crystals are hydrated and which are not.

Procedure:

1. Look at some bits of Epsom salt under a magnifying glass. Notice that they have a definite crystal shape with chisel-point ends and some light passes through them.

2. Pour a teaspoon of Epsom salt into the first test tube/glass.

3. Heat the test tube for about 30 seconds (if using a hot plate, for a few minutes). Notice if any moisture collects at the upper end of the test tube/glass. (If using a test tube, make sure you keep it slanted and not pointed at anyone.)

CRYSTALS

Results:

When Epsom salt is heated, moisture comes out of the crystals as water vapor or steam and collects at the upper end of the test tube/glass. The Epsom salt compound changes to a white flaky powder of colorless crystals that are too small to see with a magnifying glass. Without the water the crystals are much smaller, so the water was an important part of the initial crystal.

Procedure (continued):

4. Look at some table salt grains under a magnifying glass. Notice that the crystals are cubic shaped and that some light goes through them.

5. Put a teaspoon of salt into the second test tube/glass.

6. Heat the salt in the test tube for about 30 seconds (if using a hot plate, for a few minutes). Notice if any moisture comes out of the salt and collects at the upper end of the test tube/glass. (If using a test tube, make sure you keep it slanted and not pointed at anyone.)

Results:

No moisture or very little moisture is given off when the salt is heated. The crystals are still the same cubic shape after heating but now look whiter because they reflect much more of the light.

Comparison Results:

Epsom salt had large amounts of water tied up in their crystals, but table salt did not.

CRYSTALS

ACTIVITY 28
Copper Penny Colors

For this activity, you will need:
- apron
- eye protection
- 4 small paper cups
- sink
- tap water
- household ammonia cleaner
- 4 shiny pennies
- vinegar
- rubber gloves
- dishwashing liquid
- hard-boiled egg
- pen or pencil

Procedure:

1. Wear an apron and eye protection.

2. Wash the pennies with dishwashing liquid to remove any oils or dirt on the coins and rinse well.

3. Place each penny in a separate paper cup, and label the cups #1-4.

4. Drip enough vinegar on penny #1 to just cover it.

5. Drip enough ammonia cleaner on penny #2 to just cover it.

6. Separate the egg white from the egg yolk and mash up the egg white.

123

7. Place the egg white in paper cup #3 and press penny #3 into it, if possible covering the top of the penny too.

8. Drip enough water on penny #4 to just cover it.

9. Place the cups in a warm space overnight.

10. Next day examine the pennies after the top surfaces have dried out. You may need to turn the egg-white penny over. What colors have developed?

Results:

In this activity the copper surfaces of the pennies begin to react with chemicals and turn different colors.

These colors are caused by crystals that have formed but are too small to be seen without magnification. All the pennies should be discolored except penny #4.

Greenish patches form on penny #1, but the liquid is olive-green or yellow. The colors come from copper reacting with vinegar acid.

Penny #2 may have some dark splotches but the liquid is blue. The blue color comes from copper reacting with ammonia.

Penny #3 forms reddish and/or black patches. The colors come from copper reacting with sulfur in the egg white.

Penny #4 should not change color because copper does not react with water, if it is pure.

If you wait several more days and keep the pennies moist, some of the colors will continue to change as the chemical reactions continue.

Chapter 25

How Soaps Work

SOAP CHEMISTRY

When your hands or clothes get dirty, you can often just brush off the dirt or you can use water to attach to the dirt and rinse it away.

If you can't get rid of it that way, it is probably being held in place by a thin layer of grease or oil. Grease and oil do not dissolve in water or even mix with it well. Because of this, water doesn't attach well to the greasy dirt and it doesn't rinse off. Something must be done to make it so water can mix with, and attach to, the grease and oil.

Soap is often used for that purpose. Soaps have the ability to make grease and oil mix better with water. Some detergents work the same way soaps do, but other detergents clean in other ways, so we will just talk about soap here.

Soaps are made of long molecules. One end, "the head," of a soap molecule is water-loving. This just means that end of the molecule is attracted to water molecules. We will leave the question of how that works for later studies. You could say that the head end is "anchored" in the water, so that a soap molecule will be carried along with the water.

The other end of the soap molecule, "the tail," is grease-loving and tends to be attracted to oil and grease molecules. Here is a very simplified way of picturing that.

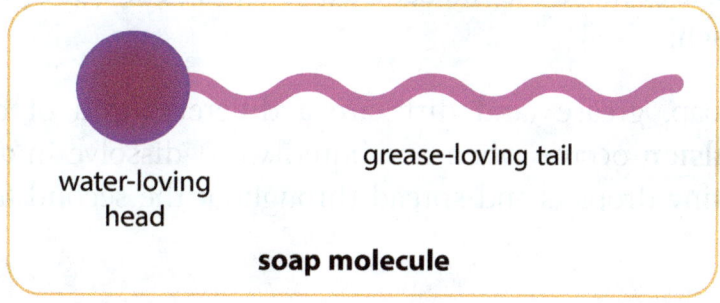

HOW SOAPS WORK

When you use soap to clean away dirt, the grease-loving tails of the molecules surround or pull on the bits of greasy dirt. Because the heads of these soap molecules are pulled along with the water, it all floats off in the water.

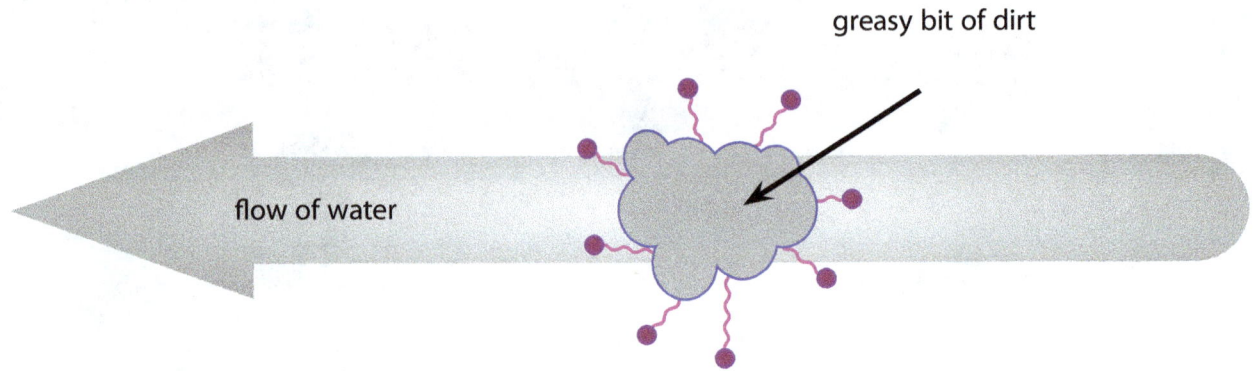

The tails of soap molecules pull on bits of grease or oil. The heads are pulled by the water. In this way greasy dirt can be broken up into droplets and carried away in the water.

You could say that the soap molecules form a sort of "bridge" connecting the oily particles to the water molecules.

When soapy water is used to clean up dirt and grease, the soap molecules attach to the dirt and grease, but the other ends of the soap molecules are attracted to the water molecules. This results in breaking up the dirt and grease into the tiny particles or droplets that spread out evenly in the water.

We earlier talked about how different molecules, evenly mixed with each other, form what is called a solution. An example is when you dissolve sugar or salt in water. The molecules completely dissolve (float freely and separately).

The liquid stays clear because the molecules are not big enough to reflect or block the light passing through.

The droplets of soap, grease (and dirt) are a different kind of mixture called an emulsion. An **emulsion** occurs when one liquid won't dissolve in another liquid, but is broken up into tiny droplets and spread throughout the second liquid.

These droplets will tend to block some of the light and the liquid is no longer clear. In this case, grease won't dissolve in water, but (with the help of soap) it gets broken up into tiny droplets and spread throughout the water. This emulsion will usually look grey.

(Milk is another example of an emulsion. Milk contains many things, but some of the droplets in milk do not dissolve and are big enough to reflect the light away, making the milk look white.)

ACTIVITY 29
How Soap Works

For this activity, you will need:

- test tube or glass jar with lid
- if a test tube is used, a test tube holder (a glass or jar will do)
- cooking oil or mineral oil
- water
- dishwashing liquid
- teaspoon

Information:

In this activity, you will see how soap is used in cleaning and how an emulsion is involved.

Procedure:

1. Pour about 3 inches of water into a test tube or jar.
2. Gently add about half an inch of cooking oil or mineral oil.
3. Notice if the water and oil mix.

Results:

The oil and water do not mix. Water is at the bottom and the oil floats on top.

Procedure (continued):

4. Put your thumb or hand over the end of the test tube, or put the lid on the jar, and shake vigorously for about 5 seconds. Then place the tube in a test tube holder (or set the jar down) for a minute and watch what happens.

Results:

The oil breaks up into droplets in the water while you shake the tube, but after about a minute, the oil and water mostly separate again into two layers. They separate because oil does not easily dissolve or disperse in the water. The oil molecules and the water molecules do not particularly attract each other. It has not become an emulsion.

Procedure (continued):

5. Add ½ teaspoon of dishwashing liquid to the tube and notice what happens.

Results:

The oil and water are still in two layers, but the dishwashing liquid sinks to the bottom.

Procedure (continued):

6. Shake the tube again for about 5 seconds. Then place the tube in a test tube holder again for a minute and watch what happens.

Results:

This time you get a milky, white liquid that does not separate out into oil and water layers. It is an emulsion.

The dishwashing liquid breaks up the oil into tiny droplets and provides a sort of "bridge" between oil droplets and water molecules. This keeps the oil droplets from flowing together again. Now the water can draw the oil droplets out when it is poured.

Chapter 26

"Hard" Water

Soaps are extremely useful in life and we use them all the time. Now that you understand the general idea of how soaps work, we are going to investigate some things that interfere with soap, and what we can do about them.

Minerals are natural substances found in rocks and soil. Rain water runs over and through the ground and picks up some mineral compounds by dissolving them out of soil and rocks.

The most common minerals in water are compounds of calcium (**Ca**) and magnesium (**Mg**), and sometimes iron (**Fe**).

Water that has a lot of these minerals in it is called **hard water**. **Soft water** is water that contains low concentrations of minerals, particularly calcium and magnesium. It isn't totally clear why these names (hard and soft) are used, but we will see why the difference matters.

Water you drink and water used for washing nearly always has some minerals in it. Small amounts of minerals are okay. In fact, normally you need some in your drinking water for good health, but too much minerals of the wrong kind can cause trouble.

If there is too much in your drinking water, the water can taste salty or strange. If the mineral content is high in water that you use for washing, soap and some detergents do not clean very well and can even leave a film behind. If we understand why that is, we can learn what to do about it.

The problem is that these minerals, particularly calcium and magnesium, "attack" soap molecules by replacing some of the atoms in the soap molecule. This changes the soap molecules so that the heads do not "like" water as much as before, and so they no longer work well as "bridges" as discussed in chapter 25.

"HARD" WATER

In fact, these changed soap molecules don't even stay dissolved as well in water and can stick to containers, pipes, clothing, etc., in the form of what is called soap scum. So instead of helping to clean, in hard water soap can become part of the problem!

Since soap scum does not "like" water as well, it does not rinse away easily. When it leaves deposits on clothing, it can make fabric feel stiff (perhaps this is why it is called "hard" water). It also can leave scum on faucets and scummy rings on the inside of bathtubs, in sinks and in washing machines.

If you wash your hair with water that has a lot of minerals in it, your hair may not come out clean and can feel sticky. If there are a lot of minerals in water, the scum can even form rock-hard materials in pipes that can clog up plumbing over time (another possible reason for "hard").

Soap makes lots of bubbles in soft water, but not in hard water. This is because the minerals combine with the soap before the soap molecules have a chance to do their work.

"HARD" WATER

Detergents work better than soap in hard water, but that still is not as good as using water with few minerals. If you have showered in an area that has hard water, you probably noticed that the soap doesn't work as well and you need to use more.

MAKING HARD WATER "SOFTER"

There are several ways to make hard water softer by removing minerals from water.

One way is to add other chemicals that combine with the minerals in the water and keep them from causing trouble with the soap molecules. Examples are washing soda and Borax™ laundry powder, which are added to laundry water. They "capture" some of the minerals, thus enabling the soap to do its job in washing the clothes.

Another way is to use a water softening unit that takes some of the calcium and magnesium minerals out of the water. If the calcium and magnesium can be "pulled out" of the water before the soap is used, the soap can work properly.

So—how to pull the minerals out? Actually the idea is to substitute sodium (**Na**) for the calcium (**Ca**) and magnesium (**Mg**) in the water. It might seem that this wouldn't help, but actually sodium doesn't cause as much trouble with soap as the others.

So water softening units do something that can seem almost magical—they use a large number of small plastic beads to swap sodium for both calcium and magnesium. The beads grab the **Ca** and **Mg** and release **Na**. This illustration gives the idea, but just shows a few beads:

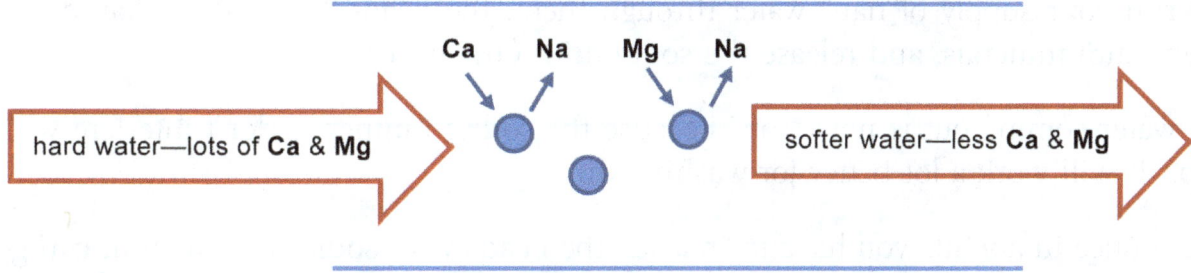

beads replacing Ca and Mg with Na

The secret here is that these beads are designed to hold on to minerals, but they hold on to calcium and magnesium more strongly than they hold on to sodium.

"HARD" WATER

So, to make this work, first the beads are loaded up with a lot of sodium (we'll see how in a moment). Then, when the water runs by, the beads grab the calcium and magnesium, and the sodium jumps off of the beads and replaces the calcium and magnesium in the water.

A simple idea, isn't it? But how do you load the beads with sodium in the first place?

Here is where knowing chemistry comes in handy!

Remember that table salt is sodium and chlorine (**NaCl**). When you dissolve salt in water (**H₂O**), the **Na** and **Cl** drift apart as ions.

$$H_2O + NaCl \longrightarrow Na^+ + Cl^-$$

So if you run a very concentrated salt solution over your beads, the beads grab the sodium. And they can hold a *lot* of sodium. This is called loading the unit.

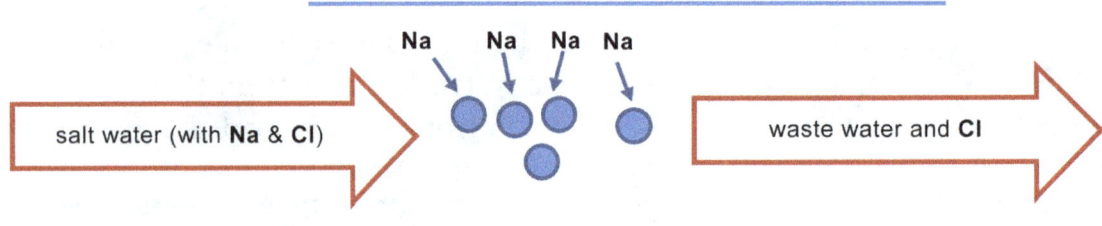

Using salt water to "load" a water softener, preparing it for use

Now when you put thousands of these loaded beads into your water softening unit and run your supply of hard water through them, the beads "grab" the calcium and magnesium minerals, and release the sodium into the water.

The water coming out is now "soft" because the sodium minerals don't interfere with soap. It will work a lot better for washing things.

(Every once in a while you have to "reload" the beads with sodium so the unit can go on working.)

ACTIVITY 30
Make Water Softer

For this activity, you will need:
- liquid soap (not detergent)
- marker
- measuring spoons
- Epsom salt
- measuring cup
- quart jar or bottle with cap
- 4 jars ½ pint or larger (same size) with tops
- Borax™ laundry power
- distilled water
- washing soda

Information:

In this activity, you will see how hard water affects soap suds, and then what happens when you add a chemical that acts as a water softener.

Procedure:

Part 1: Make Soapy Water and Hard Water

1. Add 1 tablespoon of liquid soap to the quart jar or bottle.

2. Fill the jar/bottle over half full with distilled water.

3. Screw a cap on the jar/bottle and shake it until the soap dissolves and the liquid looks milky.

4. Add ½ cup soapy water to each of the four jars.

5. Now make some "hard water." Fill the measuring cup with 1 cup of hot water. Then add 1 teaspoon Epsom salt and stir with the spoon until it dissolves.

"HARD" WATER

Part 2: Testing the Water

1. Label the first jar "#1 soapy water" and set it aside.

2. Label the other three jars #2, #3 and #4. Add 1 tablespoon of the Epsom salt water to each of these. Then notice what happens next.

Results:

In the three jars where you added Epsom salt water, the clear water gets cloudy, even after it sits for a few minutes. The cloudiness is soap scum. The scum is made of soap molecules that have been changed by the magnesium mineral in the Epsom salt.

Procedure (continued):

3. Stir or shake jar #1 (soapy water) to see if you can make bubbles. Then do the same for jar #2 (soap and hard water). Notice which one makes more soap bubbles.

Results:

You can make more soap bubbles in the soft water (jar #1) than in the hard water (jar #2). The soap has been made less effective by the hard water.

Procedure (continued):

4. Add ½ teaspoon of Borax laundry powder (4.3 grams) to jar #3 and stir until dissolved. (Here you are using Borax as the water softener.)

5. Rinse the spoon. Then add ½ teaspoon of washing soda (6.4 grams) to jar #4 and stir until dissolved. (Here you are using washing soda as the water softener.)

6. Rinse the spoon again. Then stir or shake each jar and see if you can make soap bubbles. (Stir jar #1 first, then #2, then #3 and #4.) Notice which produces the most bubbles and which produces the least.

Results:

Jar #1 (soapy water) produces the most bubbles. Jar #2 (soap and hard water) produces the least. Jars #3 and #4 (soap, hard water and water softeners) should produce more bubbles than #2.

Adding a water softener captures some of the hard water minerals, so that most of the soap molecules are still available for cleaning and are not turned into soap scum.

Chapter 27

Oxygen and Carbon Dioxide

As we know, the air consists of a mixture of several different gases. Although we breathe all those gases in and out, only the oxygen and the carbon dioxide are affected in what the body does with that breath.

People need oxygen to "burn up" (oxidize) the food they eat. Oxygen is absorbed in the lungs and transferred to the bloodstream. In various places in the body, oxygen combines with molecules from the food we eat (oxidation reactions) to produce energy and to help create other molecules for growth.

Nearly all living things need oxygen to live and grow. (There are a few kinds of microbes that live where there is no air, such as in mud or in the intestines of animals, that do not require oxygen.)

After these various oxidation reactions, much of the oxygen (O_2) breathed in eventually ends up in carbon dioxide (CO_2) molecules that get breathed out.

So, we breathe in oxygen gas and a small amount of carbon dioxide. We breathe out less oxygen and more carbon dioxide gas as a waste product. The other gases in the air just get breathed in and out.

Almost all living things take in oxygen, use it in oxidation reactions, and give off carbon dioxide gas as a waste product. This whole process is called **respiration**.

Many animals do it by breathing. Plants commonly do it by directly absorbing oxygen from the air and releasing carbon dioxide. (As we will see in the next chapter, green plants *also* do something very different during daylight.)

OXYGEN AND CARBON DIOXIDE

Some animals, such as fish and insects, have other ways of absorbing oxygen from the air and releasing carbon dioxide. All of that is respiration.

Either through respiration or other activity, living things are continuously "messing with" the amounts of oxygen and carbon dioxide in the air around them. However, it is critically important to life on Earth that the basic make-up of the air, as discussed in chapter 11, not get changed much from the percentages given there.

How is that balance maintained? The living world has evolved so that its chemistry does just that—it keeps the make-up of the air balanced very close to the percentages listed in chapter 11.

We will look first at an example of an organism (a living thing) that tends to increase the CO_2. In the next chapter, we will look at the main thing (hinted at above with plants) that helps balance the O_2 and the CO_2.

CHANGING SUGAR INTO ALCOHOL AND CARBON DIOXIDE

Yeasts are tiny, plant-like living things that use sugar for food and are cousins to the molds that grow on stale bread.

Yeast cells take in sugar molecules and give off CO_2 in two different ways. First is regular respiration, taking in oxygen and oxidizing the food (sugar in this case). This is how the yeast cells grow, just like people.

But then yeast cells also take in other sugar molecules and use a different reaction to convert them into alcohol and give off even more CO_2. This second process is an example of a kind of reaction called **fermentation**.

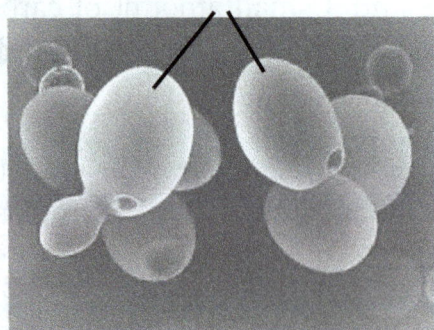

yeast cells under the microscope—they often have buds growing off the main cells

Wine and beer are made using yeast fermentation, but fermentation also has other uses.

Many breads and other pastries use yeast to make the dough rise. The yeast cells ferment sugar in the dough and produce carbon dioxide gas bubbles. The gas bubbles are trapped in the dough and cause it to rise. Alcohol also is produced, but it evaporates when the bread is baked. (By the way, this is a different process than the one mentioned earlier in the book about baking soda helping dough rise. Baking soda reacts with other chemicals in the dough to produce carbon dioxide. Yeast is a living thing that "eats" sugar and gives off carbon dioxide and alcohol.)

OXYGEN AND CARBON DIOXIDE

ACTIVITY 31
Make Alcohol and Carbon Dioxide with Yeast

For this activity, you will need:
- sugar and warm water or alternatively fruit juice and microwave oven
- packet or teaspoon of dried yeast (for baking)
- measuring spoons
- small pan
- glass or jar
- hot water

Information:

In this activity you will see how fermentation turns sugar into alcohol and carbon dioxide gas.

Procedure:

Do #1a *or* #1b. Then continue with #2:

1a. Dissolve a teaspoon of sugar (8 grams) in 5 tablespoons of warm tap water in a glass (or jar).

   or

1b. Add 5 tablespoons of fruit juice to a glass (or jar) and warm it up in a microwave for 10 to 15 seconds.

2. Pour 1/2 packet of dried yeast into the glass, **or** measure out 1 teaspoon of dried yeast (3 grams) and pour it into the glass.

3. Stir in the yeast until most of it dissolves.

4. Place the glass in a pan of hot water.

5. Let it sit for an hour. Observe what is happening after 15 minutes, after 30 minutes and 60 minutes. Also sniff the liquid each time and note any odors.

Results:

After you add yeast to a warm liquid containing sugar, the yeast cells begin to grow and break down the sugar.

After about half an hour, a sponge-like mat of carbon dioxide bubbles and yeast cells forms, and in a very warm room might overflow the container.

Alcohol is beginning to accumulate in the liquid, but some of it comes out as a gas as well. It has a smell like bread, and often by 60 minutes you may be able to notice the smell of alcohol as well.

Chapter 28

Oxygen from Plants

In the last chapter it was mentioned that nearly all living things use up oxygen and produce carbon dioxide as waste products.

If that is true, you might wonder what keeps us from running out of oxygen and filling up the air with carbon dioxide. Luckily for us, green plants can do something that animals can't do—they can produce oxygen while eating up carbon dioxide.

Although green plants do take in oxygen and give off carbon dioxide just like animals do (normal respiration), they *also* do something very different during the day when the sun shines on them.

Even while respiration is going on in the plant, another process called photosynthesis is going in the opposite direction.

Photosynthesis is a reaction in green plants that takes place when sunlight hits **chlorophyll**, the green coloring in the plant. *Photo* means "light" and *synthesis* means "putting together." In photosynthesis, sunlight puts together carbon dioxide and water to create sugar and oxygen.

This reaction uses up carbon dioxide and combines it with water to make food for the plant, and *produces 5 to 10 times more oxygen than the plant is using up in respiration!*

All the plants doing this all over the world make it possible that we have extra oxygen for people and animals to breathe.

OXYGEN FROM PLANTS

Here's how photosynthesis works.

Chlorophyll has very special qualities. The chlorophyll molecule can trap energy from sunlight. It can then use the energy to enable the plant to carry out a chemical reaction that uses carbon dioxide, and produces oxygen and food for the plant.

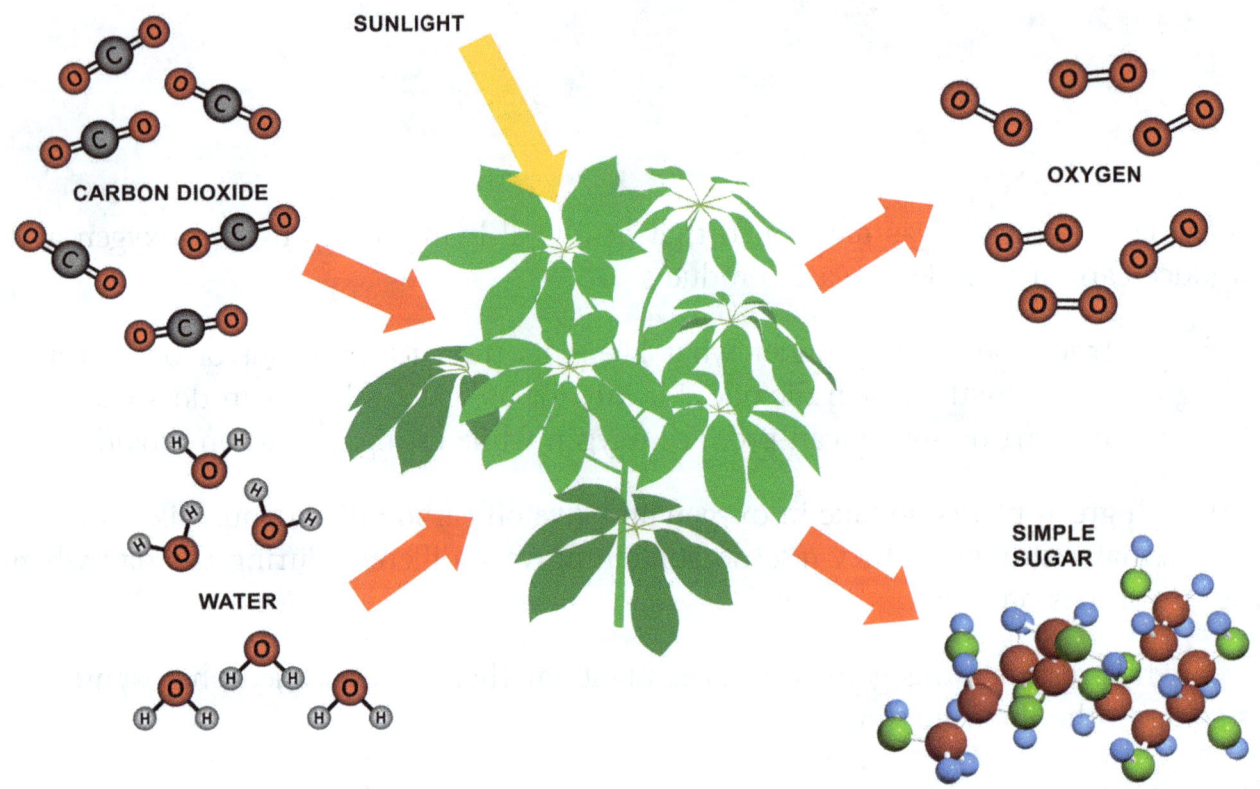

Photosynthesis in green plant during daylight.
The oxygen goes into the air and the sugar is used by the plant to grow.

What you see here is a simple reaction with carbon dioxide and water as ingredients and oxygen and sugar as products. However this reaction will not naturally occur without some help. This is where the chlorophyll and the sunlight come in.

In chapter 14 you learned about catalysts—chemicals that help a reaction occur without themselves getting used up in the reaction. Chlorophyll is such a catalyst, but with a twist.

In the absence of sunlight, chlorophyll *does not* catalyze photosynthesis. However, when a chlorophyll molecule absorbs energy from the sun, it temporarily shifts one of the electrons in the molecule and converts the chlorophyll briefly into a catalyst.

As long as the sunlight is hitting that molecule of chlorophyll, it keeps catalyzing the chemical reaction shown above.

It takes the carbon dioxide and water molecules, and transforms them into simple sugar molecules that have 6 carbons. (Table sugar molecules are not simple sugars—they have 12 carbons.) Plants then use this simple sugar as food to grow with.

But now comes the magic (for us) part of the chemical reaction. The other product of the photosynthesis reaction is oxygen, which comes off into the air as oxygen gas. As noted above, a lot more oxygen is produced than the plant's respiration is using up. And this is very fortunate, as it helps keep oxygen available for the rest of us living creatures.

You may have heard that carbon dioxide is considered a pollutant (something that pollutes—adds harmful materials to the environment). However, the above shows that plants need carbon dioxide to live and grow, so carbon dioxide by itself is not a pollutant. It is *excess amounts* of carbon dioxide in the air that can be considered a pollutant.

During photosynthesis, the oxygen molecules float off into the air. Most of the oxygen stays in the air, but eventually some of the oxygen molecules dissolve in water, such as in rivers, lakes and streams. There it is used in the respiration of the creatures that live in water.

Now here is the chemistry that's going on.

When it is receiving sunlight, the "recipe" by which the chlorophyll converts carbon dioxide and water into oxygen and simple sugar is this:

OXYGEN FROM PLANTS

For every 6 molecules of carbon dioxide and 6 molecules of water, there are produced 6 oxygen molecules and 1 simple sugar molecule (6 carbons).

Here is our illustration again:

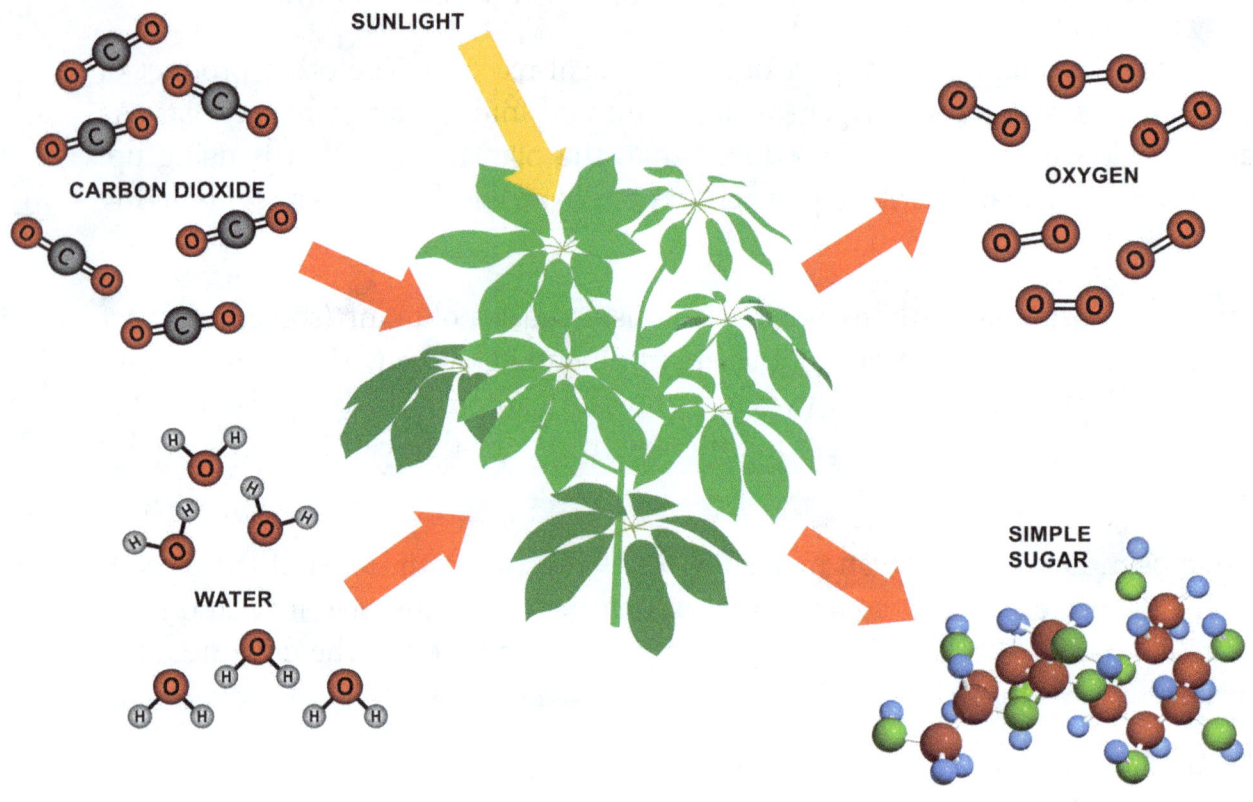

And here is the reaction diagram:

$$6\ CO_2\ +\ 6\ H_2O\ +\ \text{sunlight}\ \longrightarrow\ 6\ O_2\ +\ C_6H_{12}O_6$$
(a simple sugar)

Inspect the diagram to ensure the same numbers of each atom appear on both sides. Notice that chlorophyll does not appear in this diagram because it is a catalyst and is not actually used up in the reaction.

ACTIVITY 32
Oxygen from Plant Leaves

For this activity, you will need:

- transparent beaker or cup, about 1 cup (250 mL)
- a fresh, bright-green, thin leaf such as spinach (preferred), leaf or butter lettuce (many others may do as well)
- measuring cup
- magnifying glass
- water
- bright lightbulb on a stand
- liquid dish soap or detergent
- baking soda
- 10 mL syringe without needle (an oral syringe from a pharmacy is just right)
- plastic soda straw, not too narrow
- spoon or other mixing implement
- aluminum foil
- timer
- paper and pencil

Information:

In this activity, you will watch some plants produce oxygen gas through photosynthesis.

Procedure:

1. Select a bright green leaf to use. Optional: Before the next steps, at least briefly wrap the leaf in foil or otherwise remove it from the light. This will briefly stop the photosynthesis going on in the leaf.

2. Prepare a water solution: Put about 3/4 cup of water in the cup or beaker and add a *small* pinch of baking soda (this is to supply the leaves with carbon dioxide) and

a *small* drop of soap (this is to help the water connect to the leaves). Stir gently to avoid suds.

3. Prepare small disks of your leaf with the straw: Holding the leaf against your finger, press the straw into it so that it cuts small disks, like a hole-punch. Make about 10 disks—let them collect in the straw.

4. Float the disks inside the syringe: Pull the plunger out of the syringe and gently blow the disks from the straw into the syringe and tap them down toward the tip. Re-insert the plunger and push it most of the way down, without crushing the disks. Draw a few mL of your water solution from the cup into the syringe. Turn it upright (plunger down) and notice that the disks float. That is because there is some trapped air between the cells of the leaf.

5. We don't want this air in the leaves confusing things, so next is to "vacuum" the air out of the disks. That way, as the activity goes along, the only gas around the disks will be the newly produced oxygen. So here are the steps to do that:

    a) Press in the plunger just enough to get rid of almost all of the air inside without crushing the disks.

    b) Put your thumb over the syringe tip and create suction by gently pulling the plunger out a few mL. You should see some bubbles coming from the leaves. Hold for 10-20 seconds and gently release.

    Tap the syringe to get the bubbles off the leaves and release them up toward the tip.

    c) The disks may start to sink right away, or you may have to repeat the suction up to ten or more times, tapping after each time. They should all sink when you have pulled the air out of the leaf disks.

6. Keeping the tip of the syringe up, hold it over the prepared cup and carefully draw out the plunger and spill the liquid and disks into the cup of liquid. The disks should sink.

7. Let photosynthesis occur by exposing the disks to light by placing the bright bulb very near. Start your timer. With a magnifying glass, watch tiny bubbles appear on the disks and around the edges. These bubbles are pure oxygen being produced by the leaves. Note down when the pieces start to rise and how long it takes for all of them to rise.

(Optional extra steps)

8. Remove the light source—put the cup in the dark or wrap it in foil.

9. Check it after a while, and see that the disks have sunk again. This is because, like nearly all living things, the leaves also *use* oxygen in their respiration. So they use up the tiny bubbles during the "night." The important thing is that during daylight they make more than they use. (You can use your light to make them rise again—another "day" dawns.)

Chapter 29

Electricity in Chemistry

ELECTRICITY CAN BREAK APART WATER MOLECULES

We know that the water molecule contains hydrogen and oxygen. We are going to explore reactions where hydrogen gas and oxygen gas react to form water, and *also* reactions where water molecules are taken apart to form hydrogen and oxygen gases.

We'll start with the second reaction because we need to make some hydrogen. (We probably don't have a container of hydrogen gas sitting around!)

One thing we will see is that energy is involved in these reactions. In fact, in this reaction, we will see that quite a bit of energy comes out, in the form of heat, light and even a bit of sound!

$$\text{hydrogen gas} + \text{oxygen gas} \longrightarrow \text{water} + \text{energy}$$

One thing that tells us is that if we want to do the opposite reaction:

$$\text{energy} + \text{water} \longrightarrow \text{hydrogen gas} + \text{oxygen gas}$$

we are going to have to find a way to put energy *into* the reaction. And that is exactly where we start.

Since the first reaction above gives off heat, light and sound, we could perhaps hope that if we take some water and heat it up and shine some light on it and yell at it, it might turn into the gases! But of course it doesn't work that way. Those aren't the right forms of input energy needed.

We are going to put *electrical* energy into the water to drive our reaction.

ELECTRICITY IN CHEMISTRY

A battery produces electrical energy in the form of electrical current (flowing electrons) that can be used to run motors, light up light bulbs, and so on. (That energy actually comes from chemical reactions in the battery, but we aren't concerned with that here.) The electrical energy that a battery provides can be used to make our reaction take place.

There are good practical reasons to want to break water down into these gases.

Hydrogen can be burned for fuel, and is much cleaner than most other fuels.

Pure oxygen can be used to make fires burn much hotter. Pure oxygen also is compressed in tanks and used by divers for breathing underwater, and by people who have trouble breathing enough oxygen on their own. It has many industrial uses as well.

Using electricity to break down substances into simpler chemicals is called **electrolysis** (-*lysis* means split up, come apart or decompose).

Electrolysis can be demonstrated easily with a battery, two wires and a water solution that conducts electrical current.

ENERGY

Chemical reactions often involve some change in energy—things get warmer, things get colder, electrical energy is involved (going into the reaction or coming out), light is involved, etc.

Chemistry is part of a great many kinds of changes in the material around us and many chemical changes use or produce energy.

ELECTRICITY IN CHEMISTRY

ACTIVITY 33
Split Water Molecules with Electricity

For this activity, you will need:
- 2 6-v batteries (a 12-volt DC transformer could also be used)
- 3 connector wires (at least 1 ft. long) with alligator clips attached to both ends
- 2 #2 pencils
- bowl
- warm tap water
- table salt
- scissors

Information:

In this activity, water molecules are split into hydrogen and oxygen molecules using graphite rods as conductors.

Graphite is a form of carbon that is black and grey, and conducts electricity. It doesn't react with water. An everyday source of graphite rods is the lead in pencils.

Procedure:

1. Remove the erasers from both pencils. To do this, use scissors to cut off the metal sleeves that hold the erasers on. Then sharpen both ends of both pencils and expose enough lead for the clips to attach to. These are your graphite rods.

2. Wire connections:

   a) Clip one wire from the **−** terminal of one battery to the **+** terminal of the other.

   b) Clip a second wire from the other **−** battery terminal to one end of a graphite rod.

   c) Keeping the rods separated, clip the third wire from the remaining **+** battery terminal to the end of the other graphite rod.

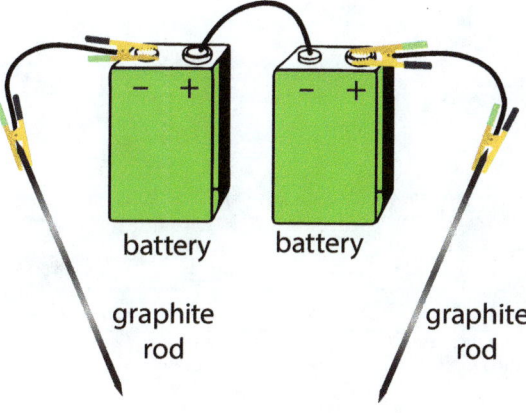

153

ELECTRICITY IN CHEMISTRY

3. Fill the bowl half full with warm water and add a pinch of salt to help the flow of electricity.

4. Hold the tips of the rods in the bowl of water so that the tips are covered with water but are not touching each other. Wait for a few seconds and watch what happens.

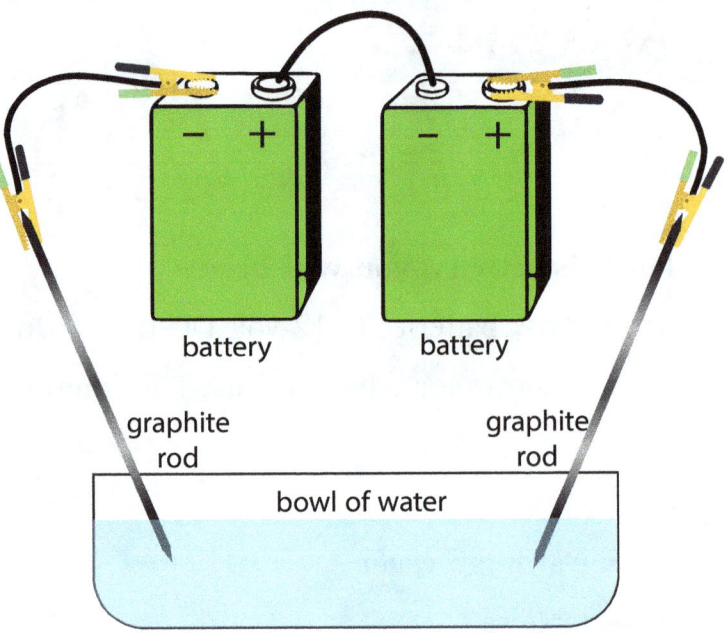

Results:

Gas bubbles begin forming on the graphite rods, about twice as much on one rod as the other. Hydrogen gas is produced at one rod and oxygen is produced at the other rod.

Recall that there are 2 hydrogen atoms in a water molecule for every 1 oxygen atom, so the gas produced in greater abundance should be hydrogen.

ELECTRICITY IN CHEMISTRY

ACTIVITY 34
Use Electricity to Collect Hydrogen Gas

For this activity, you will need:
- apron
- protective eyewear
- disposable rubber or plastic gloves
- test tube
- 3 connector wires (at least 1 ft. long) with alligator clips attached to both ends
- bowl or other container large enough to lay the test tube flat inside
- 2 insulated copper wire stiff enough to hold its shape (about 1 ft. long)
- 2 6-v batteries (a 12-volt DC transformer could also be used)
- wire stripper or knife
- tap water
- pen or pencil
- table salt
- teaspoon
- tape
- matches or lighter

Information:

Hydrogen and oxygen can be produced by electrolysis in larger amounts than the last activity, but special equipment is required that uses higher voltages or much more electrical current.

In order to create a somewhat larger flow and capture enough hydrogen to burn, we are going to change our equipment and use a different reaction.

We are still splitting the water molecules to release the hydrogen gas, but the oxygen goes into a different reaction rather than being released as gas.

ELECTRICITY IN CHEMISTRY

The oxygen reacts with copper wire and salt in the water, and produces a toxic chemical called copper chloride in the water, so you should wear disposable gloves and use eye protection.

Procedure:

A. Producing Hydrogen Gas

1. Put on an apron, and eye protection in case of splashes.

2. Fill the container with water about 3 inches deep and stir in 2 teaspoons of salt.

3. If you haven't done so already, use a wire stripper or knife to remove about 2 inches of insulation from each end of the stiffer copper wires.

4. Clip one connector wire from the – terminal of one battery to the + terminal of the other.

5. Take one of the copper wires and wind one exposed end of it around a pencil or pen a few times to make a curl. The curl needs to be small enough to fit in a test tube. Then remove the pencil or pen.

6. Lay the test tube on its side in the basin to completely fill it with water. If any air bubbles get trapped in the tube, remove them by raising the mouth end of the test tube slightly (while still keeping it under water) and tapping the tube.

7. Keeping the test tube in the water, slide the curled end of the wire into the test tube so that all of the exposed copper wire at one end is inside the tube.

8. Raise the closed end of the test tube to a vertical position in the water without letting any air bubbles get into the test tube. While doing that bend the outside wire sharply upward alongside the tube.

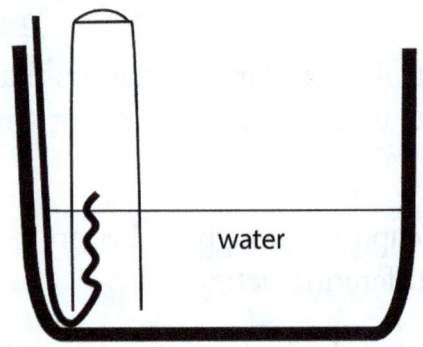

This is how the test tube and wire should be set up in the container after step #8

156

ELECTRICITY IN CHEMISTRY

9. Stand the test tube against an edge of the container and tape it upright so the copper wire is sticking out of the bowl.

10. Clip a connector wire between the - terminal of the battery and this copper wire.

11. Put on protective gloves.

12. With the third copper wire, bend one bare end at right angles and arrange it so the bent part rests on the bottom of the bowl and tape it in place.

13. Connect the other end of the third copper wire to the + terminal of the second battery. It should now be producing hydrogen gas. Check this by making sure bubbles are streaming off the wire inside the tube. Then leave it in place until at least an inch of gas accumulates in the test tube. This will take 5–10 minutes. Notice that the water in the bowl changes color as the electrolysis reaction continues.

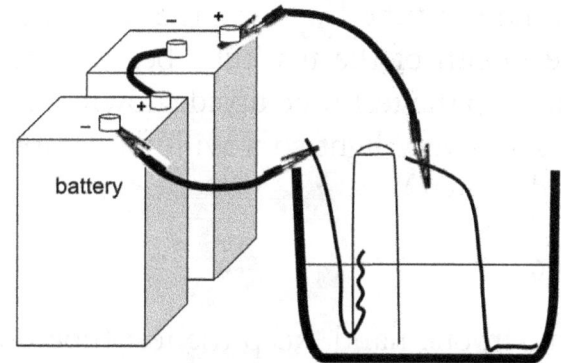

This is how it looks after step #13.

Results:

Small bubbles of hydrogen stream off the wire inside the tube and collect at the top (the closed end of the tube). At the same time, chlorine is produced at the other wire from the salt in the water.

Remember that table salt is sodium chloride (**NaCl**), and when it is dissolved in water the sodium and the chlorine drift apart as ions.

The chlorine reacts with copper from the wire and hydroxide (**OH**) from the water to produce compounds which turn the water a bluish-green color. This becomes redder or yellower as the reaction continues and other compounds are formed with the copper.

ELECTRICITY IN CHEMISTRY

(If you continue the reaction long enough, copper compounds will build up on the copper wires and slow down the reaction.)

B. Testing for Hydrogen Gas

Caution:

One of the compounds in the water is copper chloride. It is toxic and can irritate your skin, which is why to use your disposable gloves. If you get the water on your skin, wash well with soapy water.

Procedure:

1. Disconnect the wire between the two batteries. This stops the electrolysis.

2. Continue to wear protective eyewear in case the test tube breaks when you burn the hydrogen.

3. Keep protective gloves on.

4. Remove the wire from the test tube by lifting the test tube (still upside down) off the wire, but keep the mouth of the test tube below water so the water doesn't drain out and let air in. Keep the test tube upside down and set it back in the bowl. (Remember, hydrogen gas is very light so it will not escape from your test tube if you have the tube upside down.)

5. Light a match or lighter.

6. While holding the flame in one hand, keep the test tube upside down and slowly lift the test tube out of the water until it drains. Put your thumb over the opening of the test tube.

7. Turn the test tube upright, move your thumb away, and quickly bring the flame to the mouth of the test tube.

Results:

Flammability is a test for hydrogen. The gas in the tube mixes with oxygen in the air and burns with a loud "pop," showing that the gas you produced is hydrogen.

Look back through these results as see where the oxygen part of the water molecules went.

ELECTRICITY IN CHEMISTRY

More about Activities 33 and 34:

You have run two opposite activities. In the first activity you separated the water into hydrogen and oxygen. In the second part of the second activity you let them react together to make water. We did not collect the water created in the last part, but it could be done with more elaborate equipment.

Let's review the energy story here.

In the first reaction, you put energy in, using the batteries. That energy was in the form of electrical energy.

When you lit the hydrogen and got the small explosion, the energy was coming out, but it was in the form of heat, light and sound.

We can use a slightly fancier reaction diagram to show both reactions, the first going left to right and the second right to left in the diagram. The arrow pointing in opposite directions means the reaction can go from left to right *or* right to left.

$$2H_2O + energy \longleftrightarrow 2H_2 + O_2$$

Sometimes we show the energy in the diagram, sometimes not. It depends on what we want to emphasize.

If we wanted to specify what form the energy was in, we would have to separate the arrows, since the form of the energy is different in one direction than in the other.

Special Clean-up:

1. Discard the copper wires or at least the ends (they are now coated with copper compounds and no longer useful).

2. Pour the water down the sink and rinse out the basin.

3. Rinse out the test tube with water.

4. Throw away the disposable gloves in the trash.

5. Wash your hands with hand soap.

Chapter 30

Chemicals and Light

We have learned that in photosynthesis, light can be used to help make new compounds. The chlorophyll in plant cells traps energy from light and uses it to change carbon dioxide gas and water into sugar and release oxygen.

This was an example of light causing a chemical reaction to occur. Some chemical reactions go faster if light is shone on them. And of course chemical reactions can produce light as you see whenever you ignite a flame.

Some chemicals can change the light that strikes them.

A black light lamp puts out light called ultraviolet (UV) in a range you can't see with your eyes. There are some chemical substances, called **phosphors**, that will absorb the UV light and change it to light that you can see.

That is how fluorescent lightbulbs work. Electrical activity inside the tube creates a large amount of UV light. The inside of the tube is coated with phosphors which convert it into the visible light you are accustomed to.

Fluorescent lightbulbs use much less electrical power than light bulbs with a filament, so are cheaper to run when a large area needs to be lighted.

CHEMICALS AND LIGHT

ACTIVITY 35
Glow Water

For this activity, you will need:
- a black light
- tonic water in a clear glass bottle (<u>not</u> club soda or soda water). It does not need to be opened.
- room that can be darkened

Caution:
Do not look directly at the black light as it may be harmful to your eyes.

Procedure:
1. Look at the tonic water and see if you notice anything unusual.
2. Turn out the lights or go to a dim room.
3. Shine a black light on the tonic water and notice what you see.

Results:
Tonic water glows under a black light because of phosphors in the liquid.

When ultraviolet light from the black light (which humans can't see) hits the phosphors, they convert the UV light into light in the visible range, which makes the tonic water glow.

The chemicals take in one form of energy and **emit** (give off) a slightly different form of energy.

CHEMICALS AND LIGHT

ACTIVITY 36
Glowing Highlighters

For this activity, you will need:
- a black light
- sheets of white paper
- set of highlighters
- room that can be darkened

Information:

Some highlighters glow under a black light. You can use any color, but yellow is likely to work best.

Caution:

Do not look directly at the black light as it may be harmful to your eyes.

Procedure:

1. Use the highlighters and do some drawings on white paper.

2. Turn out the lights or go to a dim room.

3. Shine a black light on the paper and notice what you see.

Results:

Some of the highlighters should produce colors that glow in the dark under black light. This means their dye contains phosphors.

CHEMICALS AND LIGHT

ACTIVITY 37
Find Other Things that Glow

For this activity, you will need:

- a black light
- room that can be darkened

Caution:

Do not look directly at the black light as it may be harmful to your eyes.

Results:

There are other things that contain phosphers and will glow in the dark under black light. Take your black light to a dark room and see what you can find.

One useful application is using black light to find out where pets have urinated. Urine shows up as bright white spots under black light, even when it has dried, so you could use a black light to find it and clean it up.

U.S. paper money ($5 or greater) have strips in them that can show up in black light—this helps combat counterfeiting.

Some clothing will glow because of the dye used.

Black lights are often used in investigating crime scenes to detect blood. Blood itself does not glow, but if it is sprayed with a certain chemical, the result glows under a black light.

Chapter 31
Milk Chemistry

PLASTIC FROM MILK

Milk and milk products such as yogurt and cheese are obviously foods, but milk has chemical uses too.

Milk contains protein. And it is easy to change the protein in milk to a chemical compound called **casein** (KAY-seen). Cheese is mainly casein, but casein also can be used in making plastics, adhesives and paints.

A **plastic** is any soft material that can be shaped and will hold its shape after it has hardened. Casein was the first plastic ever made. Other than making buttons, it is not much used as a plastic today because better plastics have been invented.

USING MILK TO SHOW MOLECULAR MOTION

You may have noticed that, if you carefully fill a clean, fully dry glass with water and then *very* carefully overfill it a few drops at a time, the water can stand up slightly above the top of the glass without spilling over.

This is because the molecules at the surface hold together through mutual attraction and form a sort of "film" on the surface. This effect is called **surface tension**.

The film is not very strong and you can break it easily. Different liquids have different strengths of surface tension. One of the results of surface tension is that the surface molecules of the liquid are somewhat held in place by the film, rather than moving as freely as molecules below the surface.

MILK CHEMISTRY

This is a part of chemistry that is different from the study of chemical reactions. It is called **physical chemistry**. It studies the physical qualities of substances and how molecules behave with each other *without* having chemical reactions. Surface tension is a good example.

Milk is a liquid with a definite surface tension, and it can be used to show molecular motion. You will have a chance to see how this works in one of the following activities.

MILK CHEMISTRY

ACTIVITY 38
Make Plastic from Milk

For this activity, you will need:
- milk (nonfat milk is best)
- white vinegar or lemon juice
- glass
- tablespoon
- microwave-safe container or pan
- plate
- microwave or hot plate
- filter or filter paper, such as a coffee filter

Procedure:

1. Pour a glass of milk into a pan or microwave-safe container.

2. Heat the milk gently until it feels warm to your finger.

3. Slowly add 3 tablespoons of vinegar, or 1 tablespoon of lemon juice, while you continue to stir the milk. (Some white strands will begin to form in the liquid as the reaction starts.)

4. Continue stirring until the pieces come together.

5. Pour the mixture through a filter or filter paper and collect the solids in your hand. Squeeze out the liquid.

Results:

The milk protein comes together into a rubbery white mass which is casein. It could be used to make cheese and it is the starting point for making other chemicals.

MILK CHEMISTRY

Procedure (continued):

6. Place your lump of casein onto a plate.

7. Mold it into a shape, such as a button or a star (don't leave it too thick), and leave it to harden overnight in a warm place.

Results:

The casein plastic you made will get fairly hard, but commercial casein plastic is treated with another chemical to make it much harder.

MILK CHEMISTRY

ACTIVITY 39
Make a Milk Rainbow

For this activity, you will need:
- cup of milk *other than nonfat milk* (can be from powdered milk)
- measuring cup
- liquid soap or dishwashing liquid
- food colors: red, yellow, blue
- sink
- teaspoon
- bottle cap or similar small container
- small clean paper or plastic plate
- cotton swabs

Information:

Milk is a liquid with a definite surface tension, but some different compounds can weaken or break up the surface tension film.

In this activity, we will see that liquid soap weakens or breaks up the surface tension. The surface molecules start moving around much more and you can actually see the motion.

If you gently add drops of different food colors to the surface of milk, the colors remain separate where they are and don't mix. This is because the milk molecules in the surface film aren't moving much. However, if you add a small amount of liquid soap, the colors spread out rapidly and mix to make new colors.

Procedure:

1. Measure about a teaspoon of liquid soap into the bottle cap or similar container. Then rinse the teaspoon well in water.

MILK CHEMISTRY

2. Use the spoon to measure out or pour enough milk to completely cover the bottom of the plate with milk about ¼ inch deep.

3. Wait briefly to ensure the milk settles down. Then gently add 2 drops of red food color to the milk near the center of the plate.

4. Gently add 2 drops of yellow food color near the center of the plate so that yellow doesn't overlap with red.

5. Gently add 2 drops of blue food color near the center of the plate so the colors don't overlap.

6. Touch one end of a cotton swab to the liquid soap. Then touch it to the milk in the center of the dish and hold it there for 10 to 15 seconds. Watch what happens.

7. Pour the milk/food color mixture into the sink. Then rinse the plate off with water and dry it so that you can use it again.

8. Repeat steps 1–6 again with different amounts of food colors and touching the swab in different places. Watch what happens. Use a clean cotton swab each time you repeat the activity.

Results:

The colors initially hold fairly still in place, but when you touch the liquid soap to the milk, they suddenly move and mix, creating new colors and new patterns of color.

The molecules in the milk surface were held somewhat in place by molecular attraction (surface tension), but the liquid soap sharply reduces the tension between surface milk molecules, and they start moving about rapidly.

When the milk molecules move, they carry the food color molecules along, and when the food color molecules mix, they form different colors. The colors change because red, yellow and blue are basic paint colors, and when you mix them, they make other colors.

Chapter 32

Metal Chemistry

As we have seen, much of chemistry focuses on reactions between elements and compounds that result in changes to the compounds.

We have briefly touched on what is called physical chemistry, which studies some of the ways that atoms and molecules interact with each other *without* reacting to change the compounds.

This chapter explores that subject further. The interaction of metal atoms is a simple place to start.

Metals can simply be coated onto one another. This is called **plating**. In plating, the molecules are not mixing together, just forming a thin layer.

Metals can also be melted and mixed together. Such a mixture is called an **alloy**. In an alloy, the different kinds of molecules spread out evenly with each other, but they are not reacting with each other. You could think of it as one of the metals dissolving in the other. The metals have to be hot enough to melt for this to happen.

Steel is an example of an alloy. Steel is a mixture of iron and carbon and other metals.

United States pennies used to be made almost entirely of copper metal. Since 1982, they have been made mostly of zinc metal, which is cheaper than copper. They are coated (or plated) with a thin layer of copper.

As you'll see in the next activities, pure copper metal is reddish-brown, but when copper is coated with zinc, the surface looks like silver.

When zinc and copper are melted together, they form an alloy called **brass**, which has a golden color.

Brass has a great many uses. It is used to make gold-colored decorations, water faucets, refrigerators, locks, keys, doorknobs, bells and musical instruments such as trumpets.

METAL CHEMISTRY

ACTIVITY 40
Make "Silver" and Golden Pennies

For this activity, you will need:

Note: If you use a pan, you cannot use it for cooking because the chemicals used are poisonous.

- apron
- eye protection
- clean beaker or very small pan
- second beaker or small glass
- paper towels
- measuring cup
- water
- hot plate or gas burner
- measuring spoons
- dishwashing liquid
- zinc sulfate (from garden store)
- 4 shiny pennies
- mossy zinc (purchase online)
- tweezers

Information:

In this activity, we will start with shiny copper pennies, and coat them with zinc, making zinc plating. Then we will make the alloy brass.

To make the plating, we will use **mossy zinc**, which is small nuggets of zinc metal made by rapidly cooling molten zinc in water.

METAL CHEMISTRY

Then to make our alloy, we will heat the copper pennies and the zinc until the two metals join together to make the alloy, brass. The thin layer of brass on the surface of the pennies will make them look golden.

Remember—in the plating, the molecules are not mixing together, just forming a thin zinc layer, but in making the thin alloy layer, the molecules are actually mixing together.

Procedure:

Part 1. "Silver" Pennies

1. Put on an apron and protective eye wear.

2. Wash 4 shiny pennies with dishwashing liquid and water to clean off any oils and dirt. Then rinse them well.

3. Add 3 oz. or 6 tablespoons of hot water to a clean beaker or very small pan.

4. Add 3 level teaspoons of zinc sulfate (15 grams) to the water and stir until dissolved.

5. Spread mossy zinc in the center of the container with the zinc sulfate solution, enough to cover a 2-inch circle in the center bottom of the pan or the bottom of the beaker. This will take about a tablespoon of mossy zinc.

6. Using tweezers, place 3 cleaned-up pennies in the pan/beaker. Make sure the pennies lie on the mossy zinc but don't touch each other.

7. Place the pan/beaker on a hot plate and turn the heat all the way on and bring the solution to a boil.

8. While the solution is boiling, fill a small glass or another beaker 3/4 full with tap water. This will be your rinse water.

9. When the solution begins to boil vigorously, turn down the heat to a low boil and continue boiling for about 10-15 minutes or until the bottom of the coins become coated with a silvery coat. (You can lift the coins carefully with tweezers to check the undersides of the coins.) The pennies probably will not turn silver all at the same time.

Results:

The underside of the pennies will slowly become coated with zinc and turn a silver color. They are now zinc-plated.

METAL CHEMISTRY

Procedure (continued):

10. Turn the coins over carefully and continue boiling until both sides of the coin are covered with a silvery coat.

11. When a coin is coated with zinc on both sides, carefully remove it from the solution and rinse it in the rinse water.

12. Turn off the hot plate.

13. Place each silvery coin on a paper towel and allow it dry.

Part 2. Brass Pennies

If you have a gas burner:

1. Pick up 2 of the silvery pennies with tweezers and pass them over the flame until golden.

If you don't have a gas burner:

1. Let the hot plate cool enough to be able to touch it or use another hot plate that is already cool.

2. Make sure the hot plate surface is clean. Place 2 of the silvery pennies on the hot plate with tweezers.

3. Turn the hot plate to medium and watch what happens. This may take a few minutes.

Results:

The heat gradually spreads the zinc atoms into the copper over the entire surface of the coins to make a surface layer of golden brass.

Remember—the pennies started with only a thin layer of copper and that layer got turned into a thin layer of alloy. You will be able see the silver color turn to gold as you watch. If you are using a hot place, once a penny is a brass/golden color on one side, pick it up with tweezers and turn it over. Or pass it over the flame if using a gas burner.

METAL CHEMISTRY

Procedure (continued):

4. When the second side also has turned golden, rinse the coins and then place them on the paper towel to dry again.

5. When you are finished, turn off the hot plate or gas burner.

6. Once the 2 golden pennies have cooled, place them next to the original (unchanged) penny and your remaining silver penny, and compare the colors.

Results:

The change to a golden color is most obvious when you place a golden penny and a shiny, silver penny side-by-side and compare them.

Chapter 33

Slime

Some kinds of molecules have the ability to connect up to one another and form long chains or strands. Such a chain is a series of copies of the same basic molecule.

When a molecule will do this, the basic molecule is called a **monomer**, and when they are chained together, the whole strand is called a **polymer** (*mono-* means single or one; *poly-* means multiple or many, and *mer* means parts).

Some polymers might be just a few monomers connected together, but sometimes they can be very long—even up to 1,000 units long!

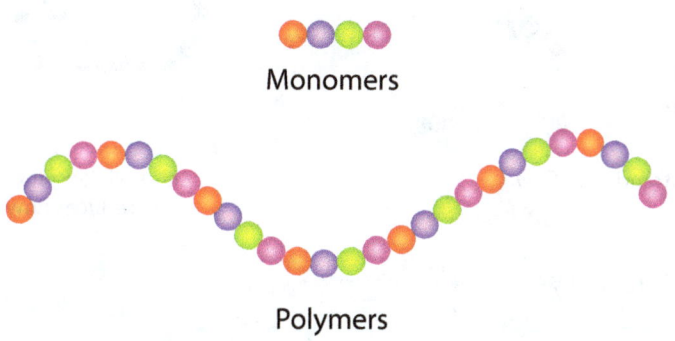

A monomer is a basic molecule.
A polymer is a long-chain molecule made up of a repeated pattern of monomers.

The basic monomer is a molecule, but it is common to consider the long chain to also be a kind of molecule. A polymer usually takes its name from *poly* + *(the monomer name)*.

So now we know about polymers. What does that have to do with slime?

SLIME

White glue is one of the ingredients in slime, and it's a polymer!

White glues are mostly made up of very long strands of molecules of a substance called polyvinyl acetate. (The monomer molecule is vinyl acetate, so the strand is poly + vinyl acetate).

When you pour white glue, the strands in the glue slide past each other. To turn it into slime, we need to get the strands not to slide as much.

Some substances can be used to cross-connect the strands so the mixture turns into a gel. A **gel** is a mixture of chemicals that looks and acts like stiff jelly.

Borax is a white crystalline mineral that is used in some laundry powders for cleaning. It contains the element boron. Borax can be used to create cross-links between the polyvinyl acetate strands of white glue. This keeps the strands from sliding past each other so easily and turns the white glue into a gel that can be used as slime!

Here is what happens at the chemical level:

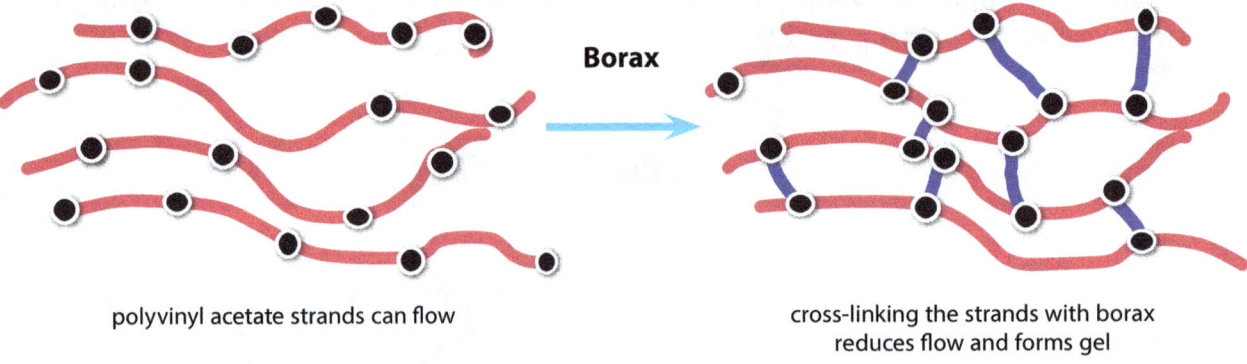

polyvinyl acetate strands can flow

cross-linking the strands with borax reduces flow and forms gel

Are you ready to give it a try?

ACTIVITY 41
Make Slime (Also Called Gak)

For this activity, you will need:
- apron
- Borax laundry powder
- tablespoon
- white glue, or polyvinyl acetate
- water
- zip-lock sandwich bag
- food color (optional)
- measuring cup or disposable cup for glue
- large glass or jar

Procedure:

1. Put on your apron and measure 1 cup of water into a glass. Then measure 1 tablespoon of Borax laundry powder and add it to the glass. Stir it until it is completely dissolved. This is your Borax-water solution.

2. Measure 4 tablespoons of white glue into a measuring cup or disposable cup.

3. Add 2 oz. of water to the measuring cup and mix thoroughly to make a watery glue solution.

4. (Optional) Add a couple drops of food coloring for color.

5. Add 1/2 cup of Borax-water to the measuring cup in small amounts while stirring.

6. Pour the mixture into a zip-lock sandwich bag.

7. Seal the bag and quickly massage the mixture to keep it all mixed together. (The mixture turns into a gel or "slime." Don't wait long or you'll just get a lump surrounded by liquid.)

8. Rinse out the measuring cup with water.

9. Take the slime out of the bag and stretch it.

Results:

When Borax is added to white glue, boron atoms form cross-links in the glue. The result is a thickened gel. It is safe to play with.

If you want to save it, keep it in a sealed bag in a refrigerator. The slime will keep for weeks in a refrigerator, but may become moldy after a week if left out. It will wash out of clothing.

Special Clean-Up:

The gel can be removed from carpets, furniture and clothing by wetting it with vinegar and then washing with soap and water.

ACTIVITY 42
Make Bouncy Slime

Repeat steps for Activity 41 Make Slime, but omit Step 3 (leave out the water). The gel produced is bouncier than regular slime.

Chapter 34

Colored Flames from Metal Compounds

Earlier we saw that burning iron produces yellow sparks. Many metals and metal compounds burn in oxygen with different colors. The flame colors are different enough that they are used to tell what kind of metal is present.

A **flame test** is a test where a metal compound or element is heated in a flame so it can be identified by the color of light it gives off.

When you heat a metal element or a compound in a flame, some of the electrons of the metal atoms soak up extra energy from the flame. When the metal or compound cools off slightly, the electrons give up that extra energy by emitting light of a certain color.

This is another example of how energy goes into atoms or chemicals in one form and then comes out in a different form—in this case, heat in and light out.

Once you know the colors, you could be given an unknown sample and figure out which metal was present from the color of the light given off.

COLORED FLAMES FROM METAL COMPOUNDS

ACTIVITY 43
Flame Tests—Colored Flames from Metals

For this activity, you will need:
- protective eye wear
- apron
- water (distilled if easily available)
- wooden coffee stirrers—5 or more
- burner (flame)
- matches or lighter
- a selection of chemicals to test (at least 5 from the list below):

Procedure:

Note: The colors will show up best in a room where the lights are dimmed.

1. Let the wooden coffee stirrers soak in water for a bit.

2. Put on an apron and eye protection.

3. Assemble all the materials you will need.

4. Turn on the burner and adjust the flame so that it is as intense as possible (blue or white).

5. Dip the tip of a wetted coffee stirrer in the first chemical. You just want a small amount of the chemical to stick to the end of it.

6. Rotate the coffee stirrer so the edge (not the flat side) is facing up.

7. Put the end of the coffee stirrer (with chemical on it) into the very top part of the flame and hold it there until the chemical catches on fire. The coffee stirrer stick will tend to burn yellow-orange, but the chemical should start burning first (that is why you wet the stick), so you are looking for the color when the chemical first starts to burn.

COLORED FLAMES FROM METAL COMPOUNDS

8. Compare the flame color you observed with the chart below.

9. Repeat steps 5 through 8 with each chemical you have. Use a clean coffee stirrer each time.

10. Repeat the tests as needed until you can do a flame test confidently.

CHEMICAL	THE METAL ELEMENT THAT BURNS	FLAME COLOR
boric acid	boron (B)	*bright green*
calcium chloride or calcium mineral supplement	calcium (Ca)	*red-orange*
copper chloride or copper sulfate	copper (Cu)	*blue-green to green*
iron powder or iron supplement	iron (Fe)	*gold*
magnesium sulfate (Epsom salt)	magnesium (Mg)	*white*
salt substitute or cream of tartar	potassium (K)	*light purple to red*
table salt	sodium (Na)	*bright yellow*
strontium chloride or flare material	strontium (Sr)	*crimson red*
zinc powder or zinc supplement	zinc (Zn)	*blue-green to pale green*

COLORED FLAMES FROM METAL COMPOUNDS

ACTIVITY 44
Flame Test Unknown Chemicals

For this activity, you will need:
- eye protection (for you and your partner)
- apron (for you and your partner)
- water (distilled if easily available)
- burner (flame)
- matches or lighter
- a selection of chemicals to test (at least 5 from the list in Activity 43)
- wooden coffee stirrers—5 or more

Procedure:

1. Have a partner secretly choose at least one of the chemicals you tested in the last activity, and pour out a small sample on a piece of paper without letting you know which one it is. If it is too obvious from the appearance of the sample, have your partner dip the stirrer in it secretly.

2. Your job then is to carry out a flame test on the sample and identify the metal element it contains. If you don't pass on the first try, repeat the test until you can clearly identify the metal from the color. Then do another one the same way.

3. When you are finished with the tests, throw the burned coffee stirrers in the trash and clean up any chemical spills.

Chapter 35

A Glance Forward

You have learned that chemistry affects or controls an enormous amount of the environment you interact with. As you learn more, you will find that this is even more true than it might seem so far.

You have seen that atoms are incredibly small, and have had a first look at the way they are structured and behave, with electrons outside of the nucleus.

This introduced the idea of electrical charge. You saw that electric charge played a role in some reactions, when ions with opposite charges attracted each other and combined into salts in neutralization reactions.

Something to look forward to learning about is that electrons and electrical charge actually play a key role in *all* chemical reactions. In the process you will learn a lot more about electrons and their behavior in atoms and between atoms. You will discover that the way electrons are arranged and behave in atoms is really the subject underlying almost all of chemistry.

You learned about the different elements but not yet about what makes one element different from another. What is it about the structure of these atoms that makes them behave so differently? What is an atom's nucleus like? As you learn about these things, much about chemistry and other things in your environment will become more understandable.

You learned about acids and bases, and caused many reactions with them, worked with indicators to test the acidity of chemicals, and learned how acids and bases can be both useful and dangerous.

A GLANCE FORWARD

All of this gives a glimpse of how people use chemistry to shape, improve and control the world around them, such as by softening water, cleaning things, making plastics, helping plants grow and capture the carbon dioxide in the atmosphere, and many other things.

You have made a good start—the start of a very rewarding journey. Enjoy it!

Appendix

More about Electrical Charge 191
    History 191
    Summary 192
Glossary 195
Materials Needed for the Activities in this Book 203

More about Electrical Charge

If you hear it said that some piece of matter has *electrical charge*, it just means that it is not neutral—that it is either positive or negative. "Negative" was the name assigned to electrons, so electrons have *negative charge*. "Positive" was the name assigned to nuclei (plural of nucleus) so they have *positive charge*.

But where did the word "charge" come from?

It was learned early on that you could start with a neutral object and do something to it, like rub it, and turn it into a negative object. Or turn it into a positive object.

Scientists concluded that somehow they were "loading" the object up with the negative characteristic or the positive characteristic. The word "charging" is an old word for *loading* and so they said they were charging an object when they caused it to become negative or positive.

So something had charge if it was negative or positive (i.e., if it had been *charged*). It was not at first known what was being loaded, just that *something* was being loaded and it could be either negative or positive.

So you can either say that something "is negative" or that it "has negative charge." These mean the same thing. Similarly for positive and positive charge. Otherwise, you just say something is neutral. The electron has negative charge, the nucleus has positive charge, and the overall balanced atom is neutral.

HISTORY

For quite a while there was no certainty about what it was that caused matter to become positive or negative. It was known that a charge could be made to flow from one object to another, but it remained unknown *what* was flowing. A big search went on in the late 1800s. Finally in 1897, English scientist J. J. Thompson discovered that what was flowing was a tiny bit of the negative type, which he named the electron.

MORE ABOUT ELECTRICAL CHARGE

Soon it was understood that matter was negative when it had more electrons, and that for matter to be positive, it just meant that it had a shortage of electrons. And when charge *flowed* from one object to another, the flowing electrons could make the receiving object negative, and the giving object positive.

You have probably experienced rubbing a balloon on a sweater and then having it stick to the sweater. That is just a basic example of the effect of electricity. Some electrons from the sweater have gotten rubbed off onto the balloon, so now the balloon is negative and the sweater is positive. And they attract each other.

The question of "what was the positive part in the nucleus" was settled later by New Zealand/English scientist Ernest Rutherford in 1917. He discovered the positive proton which resides in the nucleus of atoms. It is much larger than the electron and does not flow through matter the way electrons do.

An atom generally has the same number of protons and electrons, so the positive and negative balance each other, making the atom neutral.

SUMMARY

Positive and *negative* and *neutral* are simply terms that were invented to give a label to the three "types" of matter where

1. two bits of positive matter repel each other,

2. two bits of negative matter repel each other,

3. positive and negative bits attract each other,

4. neutral matter does not attract or repel.

Matter is said to *have a charge or be charged* if is positive or negative.

Electrons are the basic bits of negative matter.

Protons are the basic bits of positive matter.

Electrons exist in the outer layers of atoms, but sometimes also float free.

Protons exist in the centers of atoms, and stay put.

These are characteristics of matter, and we use the word *electricity* to describe this characteristic of matter.

The whole story of how electrons shift and move is very important to chemistry and almost all other branches of science.

Glossary

A

acid: a substance that has a sour, sharp or biting taste. Vinegar, lemon juice and orange juice all contain acids, but most acids are not foods and many are poisonous. What makes acids different from other chemicals is that each acid molecule contains one or more hydrogen atoms (**H**) that are loosely held onto by the molecule. When the acid is dissolved in water, these loose H's tend to drift away from the rest of the acid molecule. When the hydrogens come loose like that, they leave an electron behind with the rest of the molecule. The hydrogens become positive ions. (Ch. 15, 17 & 21)

acidic: When the acid is dissolved in water, loosely held hydrogen atoms (**H**) tend to drift away from the rest of the acid molecule. When the hydrogens come loose like that, they leave an electron behind with the rest of the molecule, so they become positive (**H⁺**) ions floating around. These hydrogen ions are free to react with other atoms or molecules. We say that this solution becomes *acidic,* which just means it has some of these loose positive hydrogen ions floating around. (Ch. 21)

alloy: a mixture of metals melted and mixed together. In an alloy, the different kinds of molecules spread out evenly with each other, but they are not reacting with each other. You could think of it as one of the metals dissolving in the other. Steel is an example of an alloy. Steel is a mixture of iron and carbon and other metals. When zinc and copper are melted together, they form an alloy called brass. (Ch. 32)

atoms: the tiny bits that make up all matter. Atoms combine in many ways to make up all the substances we encounter, like wood, water, air, bone, etc. All these substances are what we call matter. There are about 100 different kinds of atoms in nature. Some examples you have probably heard of are hydrogen, oxygen and carbon. (Ch. 2)

arrow: the arrow in a chemical reaction means "produces." (Ch. 9)

GLOSSARY

B

base, basic: the opposite of an acid is a base, a substance that has a bitter taste, and in water feels slippery. What makes bases different is that each molecule of the base has one (or more) hydrogen-oxygen (**OH**) group that are part of the molecule, but the group is not held tightly to the rest of the molecule. The OH group is called a "hydroxide group." When the base is in a water solution, these OH's tend to drift free of the rest of the molecule. They take an extra electron from the rest of the molecule and they become negative (**OH⁻**) ions floating around. These negative hydroxide ions are free to react with other atoms or molecules. We say that this solution becomes *basic*, which just means it has some of these loose negative hydroxide ions floating around ready to react. (Ch. 17 and 21)

brass: When zinc and copper are melted together, they form an alloy called brass, which has a golden color. (Ch. 32)

C

carbon: Carbon is an element that is an important part of living cells. It is also part of some minerals and rocks. Carbon, by itself, is usually a blackish solid, as found in coal, or asphalt. (Ch. 8)

carbonates: Carbonates are rocks, minerals and chemical compounds whose molecules have carbon and oxygen in them, and which react with acids to release carbon dioxide. Carbonates are common in rocks from the sea and in seashells. (Ch. 15)

casein: a chemical compound that comes from protein in milk. Cheese is mainly casein, but casein also can be used in making plastics, adhesives and paints. (Ch. 31)

catalyst: a chemical that helps a reaction between other compounds without itself getting used up. Catalysts are sort of active "spectators" to the reaction—they encourage it but don't actually get involved. (Ch. 14)

charge: Charge is the overall amount of electrical energy in an atom or group of atoms caused by too many electrons (negative) or too few electrons (positive). (Ch. 20. Also see "More about Electrical Charge" in the appendix.)

GLOSSARY

chemical: a) a pure substance that is made up of only one kind of molecule or atom. Water, carbon dioxide, gold and sugar are examples of chemicals. They are pure because all their molecules are the same. Gold, iron and aluminum are also examples of chemicals. In their cases, they are pure because all their *atoms* are the same. Their atoms don't link up to make molecules. b) A chemical is a substance made up of only one kind of molecule, but can either be an elemental substance or a compound. (Ch. 2, 5)

chemical reaction: A chemical reaction occurs when atoms and molecules actually combine (join) with each other or break apart, or both, so that different molecules, compounds and substances are formed. The new substances might be pure chemicals or mixtures. (Ch. 6 and 9)

chemistry: the scientific study of chemicals, what they are made of, their structure, and how they change when they combine or interact with other chemicals. (Ch. 1)

chlorophyll: the green coloring in a plant. The chlorophyll molecule can trap energy from sunlight. It can then use the energy to enable the plant to carry out a chemical reaction that uses carbon dioxide, and produces oxygen and food for the plant. This process is called photosynthesis. (Ch. 28)

compound substance: Molecules made up of two or more different atoms (elements) are called a compound substance or compound for short. The word compound can refer to just one molecule or many, so whether you have one molecule of water or a gallon of water or a swimming pool full, it is still the compound called water. (Ch. 5)

crystal: In some solid compounds, the molecules can line up in a regular pattern. You could say these molecules "like" to fit together in a certain repeating way. When this happens, the substance appears in regular shapes with flat surfaces. These are called crystals. (Ch. 24)

D

dilute: make a chemical weaker by adding water. (Ch. 14)

distilled water: is water that has been boiled into vapor and condensed back into water. This removes impurities. (Ch. 23)

GLOSSARY

E

electricity: Electricity is a characteristic of matter. The characteristic is that matter comes in three different kinds, which are called positive, negative and neutral. (Ch. 18)

electrolysis: Using electricity to break down substances into simpler chemicals is called electrolysis (*-lysis* means split up, come apart or decompose). (Ch. 29)

element: Each kind of atom is an element—hydrogen is an element, carbon is an element. Gold and iron are elements. Some other familiar elements are aluminum, oxygen, helium, copper and chlorine. In nature, there are about 100 different elements. When you speak, for instance, of "the element oxygen" you can mean a single atom of oxygen, a oxygen molecule of two oxygens, or a whole tankful of oxygen—it's all the element oxygen. (Ch. 4)

elemental substance: Molecules that are made up of only one kind of atom (element), such as hydrogen gas or oxygen gas, are called elemental substances. An elemental substance can also be a single atom, like iron. (Ch. 5)

emit: give off. (Activity 35, Ch. 30)

emulsion: An emulsion occurs when one liquid won't dissolve in another liquid, but is broken up into tiny droplets and spread throughout the second liquid. (Ch. 25)

F

fermentation: the reaction where yeast cells break down sugar into alcohol and carbon dioxide. (Ch. 27)

flame test: a test where a metal compound or element is heated in a flame so it can be identified by the color of light it gives off. (Ch. 34)

formula: When atoms combine to make a molecule, the molecule gets its name from the symbols of the atoms. This name is called a **formula** because it tells both what atoms and how many of each kind are there. For example, a water molecule consists of two hydrogen atoms, both linked to an oxygen atom. The formula for a water molecule is written as H_2O (pronounced "H 2 O"). The subscript $_2$ tells you that in each water molecule there are 2 hydrogen atoms. If you wanted to indicate that two water molecules were involved, you would put a 2 out front: $2H_2O$. (Ch. 13)

GLOSSARY

G

gel: a mixture of chemicals that looks and acts like stiff jelly. (Ch. 33)

graphite: is a form of carbon that is black and grey, and conducts electricity. It doesn't react with water. An everyday source of graphite rods is the lead in pencils. (Ch. 29)

H

hard water: The most common minerals in water are compounds of calcium and magnesium, and sometimes iron. Water that has a lot of these minerals in it is called hard water. (Ch. 26)

hydrated crystals: Crystals usually seem quite dry, but some types of crystals actually have water molecules tied up inside them and are known as hydrated crystals. (Ch. 24)

I

indicator: a special test substance that turns one color when it is added to a base and turns another color when it is added to an acid. (Ch. 23)

ion: When an atom or group of atoms has extra electrons or is missing some, it is no longer neutral. Then we call it charged. Charge is the overall amount of electrical energy in an atom or group of atoms caused by too many electrons (negative) or two few electrons (positive). Once an atom becomes charged, we no longer call it an atom. A charged atom or group of atoms gets a new name: **ions**. If an atom has one or more extra electrons, it is called a **negative ion**. If it has lost one or more electrons, it is called a **positive ion**. (Ch. 20)

M

material: can be used to indicate some particular kind of matter. It's not a very exact meaning, just a way to speak of particular pieces or sorts of matter. (Ch. 3)

matter: anything that has weight and takes up space. It can be solid (like wood), liquid (like water), or a gas (like air). (Ch. 2)

mineral: Minerals are natural substances found in rocks and soil. (Ch. 26)

GLOSSARY

mixture: We call the kind of substance that has various kinds of molecules a mixture. The atoms, molecules and compounds are just mixed together. We have lots of mixtures in our environment—dirt is a mixture, food is a mixture, etc. (Ch. 2, 5)

molecule: Atoms can "connect up" or stick together in groups called molecules. A molecule has at least two atoms in it. With 100 kinds of atoms to start with, and so many ways they can connect together to make molecules, there are enormous numbers of different kinds of molecules. We say that two molecules are of the same kind (or are "alike") if they both contain the same kind and number of atoms, arranged in the same way in the group. (Ch. 2)

monomer: Some kinds of molecules have the ability to connect up to one another and form long chains or strands. Such a chain is a series of copies of the same basic molecule. When a molecule will do this, the basic molecule is called a monomer, and when they are chained together, the whole strand is called a polymer (*mono-* means single or one; *poly-* means multiple or many, and *mer* means parts). (Ch. 33)

mossy zinc: small nuggets of zinc metal made by rapidly cooling molten zinc in water. (Activity 40, Ch. 32)

N

negative ion: (See *ion*.)

neutralization reaction: The overall reaction when an acid and a base react together, including the half of the reaction that produces water and the half of the reaction that produces a salt, is called a neutralization reaction. The water produced is neutral—it is neither an acid nor a base. The salt usually is neutral too. (Ch. 22)

O

oxidation: the process in which oxygen combines with other kinds of atoms or molecules. (Ch. 11)

P

pigment: a chemical that shows color. (Ch. 23)

phosphors: There are some chemical substances, called phosphors, that will absorb the ultraviolet light and change it to light that you can see. (Ch. 30)

GLOSSARY

photosynthesis: Photosynthesis is a reaction in green plants that takes place when sunlight hits chlorophyll, the green coloring in the plant. *Photo* means "light" and *synthesis* means "putting together." In photosynthesis, sunlight puts together carbon dioxide and water to create sugar and oxygen. (Ch. 28)

physical chemistry: the study of the physical qualities of substances and how molecules behave with each other without having chemical reactions. (Ch. 31)

plastic: A plastic is any soft material that can be shaped and will hold its shape after it has hardened. (Ch. 31)

plating: Metals can simply be coated onto one another. This is called plating. In plating, the molecules are not mixing together, just forming a thin layer. (Ch. 32)

polymer: Some kinds of molecules have the ability to connect up to one another and form long chains or strands. Such a chain is a series of copies of the same basic molecule. When a molecule will do this, the basic molecule is called a monomer, and when they are chained together, the whole strand is called a polymer (*mono-* means single or one, *poly-* means multiple or many, and *mer* means parts). (Ch. 33)

positive ion: (See *ion*.)

procedure: a plan for doing something, often laid out in steps to follow. In chemistry, when setting up and causing a chemical reaction, there is usually a procedure for doing it. Procedures help you to run the reaction properly. And, very importantly, they help keep you safe. They also make it possible to repeat the reaction *the same way* if you need to. (Ch. 7)

product: In chemistry, products are what is formed from a chemical reaction. (Ch. 6)

R

reaction: (See *chemical reaction*.)

reaction diagram: a way of showing a chemical reaction with the symbols of the ingredients on the left, an arrow for "the reaction" and the symbols of the products on the right. (Ch. 9)

respiration: Almost all living things take in oxygen, use it in oxidation reactions, and give off carbon dioxide gas as a waste product. This whole process is called respiration. (Ch. 27)

GLOSSARY

S

soft water: water that contains low concentrations of minerals, particularly calcium and magnesium. (Ch. 26)

solution: Mixtures where the different molecules are *evenly* mixed with each other are called solutions. The molecules of the different ingredients are freely mixing together. Usually this applies to liquids, but air is an example of a solution that is a gas. (Ch. 5)

soot: Soot is a black, greasy, powdery substance that is formed when fuels like wax, wood and oils are not burned up completely. The compounds in soot generally have some carbon left in them (i.e., that has not combined with oxygen), which is what makes them black. (Ch. 8)

surface tension: the effect that molecules at the surface of liquids hold together through mutual attraction and form a sort of "film" on the surface. (Ch. 31)

V

ventilation: circulation or change of air. (Ch. 7)

W

water vapor: invisible gaseous water. (Ch. 11)

Y

yeast: tiny, plant-like living things that use sugar for food and are cousins to the molds that grow on stale bread. (Ch. 27)

Materials Needed for the Activities in this Book

- [ ] a room that can be darkened
- [ ] hot plate
- [ ] microwave
- [ ] propane gas burner/flame
- [ ] sink or fireproof surface/tray

SUPPLIES

- [ ] microwave safe container
- [ ] 10 mL syringe without needle (an oral syringe from a pharmacy is just right)
- [ ] 2 insulated copper wire stiff enough to hold its shape (about 1 ft. long)
- [ ] aluminum foil
- [ ] apron (for you and your partner)
- [ ] batteries: 6-v (2) (a 12-volt DC transformer could also be used)
- [ ] beaker (2)
- [ ] black light
- [ ] bright light bulb on a stand
- [ ] cabbage juice indicator (commercial, such as Red Cabbage Jiffy Juice, or homemade which the students does as an optional activity)
- [ ] candles:
  - [ ] birthday candle
  - [ ] short
  - [ ] that stand by themselves (2 of them)
- [ ] clay
- [ ] cloth or sponge
- [ ] connector wires (at least 1 ft. long) with alligator clips attached to both ends: 3 of them, with alligator clips attached to both ends (at least 1 ft. long)
- [ ] cotton swabs like a Q-tip
- [ ] cotton wads
- [ ] dishwashing liquid (different types)
- [ ] disposable rubber or plastic gloves

MATERIALS NEEDED FOR THE ACTIVITIES IN THIS BOOK

- ☐ eye dropper
- ☐ filter or filter paper (like coffee filter)
- ☐ food colors; red, yellow, blue
- ☐ hammer
- ☐ lighter
- ☐ magnifying glass
- ☐ masking tape
- ☐ wooden matches
- ☐ old washcloth
- ☐ paper:
  - ☐ notebook for recording results
  - ☐ paper towels
  - ☐ sheets of white paper
  - ☐ waxed paper
- ☐ pens:
  - ☐ a set of highlighters
  - ☐ ballpoint pen with blue ink
  - ☐ marker (thin)
  - ☐ pencils #2 (2 of them)
  - ☐ permanent marker

- ☐ pennies (4 shiny)
- ☐ protective eye wear (for you and your partner)
- ☐ scissors
- ☐ sponge
- ☐ steel wool pad (not soaped) ("0000" steel wool pads is the thinnest and works best)
- ☐ tape
- ☐ test tubes and tube holder: 20 mL or larger (3 identical)
- ☐ transparent beaker or cup, about 1 cup (250 mL)
- ☐ timer
- ☐ tongs or large tweezers
- ☐ small tweezers
- ☐ white glue, or polyvinyl acetate
- ☐ wire stripper or knife
- ☐ wood splint (wooden coffee stirrer)
- ☐ wooden coffee stirrers—5 or more

DISHES

- ☐ 4 jars ½ pint or larger (same size) with tops
- ☐ bottle cap or similar small container
- ☐ bowl
- ☐ bowl or other container large enough to lay the test tube flat inside
- ☐ clean slender stick, such as a coffee stirrer

MATERIALS NEEDED FOR THE ACTIVITIES IN THIS BOOK

- ☐ cork or rubber stopper for bottle
- ☐ cups:
  - ☐ a cup
  - ☐ disposable (for glue)
  - ☐ measuring cup
  - ☐ paper cups (4 small)
- ☐ gallon container
- ☐ glass bottle (half-liter or less) used for carbonated drinks
- ☐ glasses or jars
  - ☐ 2 small, clear, heat-proof
  - ☐ 2 drinking glasses or beakers (heat resistant)
  - ☐ 1 large, clear, heat-proof
  - ☐ small but not too short
  - ☐ second beaker or small glass
- ☐ knife
- ☐ measuring spoons
- ☐ plastic bottle—500 ml or larger with lid
- ☐ plastic soda bottle—16 oz, or half-liter
- ☐ plastic soda straw, not too narrow
- ☐ plates:
  - ☐ flat glass plate
  - ☐ small clean plate
  - ☐ paper or plastic plate
- ☐ quart jar or bottle with cap
- ☐ small mouth bottle
- ☐ small pan
- ☐ spoon or other mixing implement
- ☐ zip-lock sandwich bag

FOOD

- ☐ cooking oil or mineral oil
- ☐ egg, hard-boiled
- ☐ fresh, bright-green, thin leaf such as spinach (preferred), leaf or butter lettuce (many others may do as well)
- ☐ lemon juice
- ☐ milk:
  - ☐ a cup of milk other than nonfat - can be from powdered
  - ☐ nonfat milk
- ☐ red cabbage
- ☐ slice of apple, potato or another vegetable

MATERIALS NEEDED FOR THE ACTIVITIES IN THIS BOOK

- ☐ sugar
- ☐ sugar cubes
- ☐ table salt
- ☐ tonic water in a clear glass bottle (not club soda or soda water). It does not need to be opened.
- ☐ vinegar, regular and white
- ☐ water:
  - ☐ distilled
  - ☐ tap
- ☐ yeast (packets or dried)

CHEMICALS

- ☐ antacid tablets that contain calcium carbonate (2)
- ☐ baking soda
- ☐ Borax™ laundry powder
- ☐ chemicals to test (a selection of at least 5 from this list):
  - ☐ boric acid
  - ☐ calcium chloride or calcium mineral supplement
  - ☐ copper chloride or copper sulfate
  - ☐ iron powder or iron supplement
  - ☐ magnesium sulfate (Epsom salt)
  - ☐ salt substitute or cream of tartar
  - ☐ strontium chloride or flare material
  - ☐ zinc powder or zinc supplement
- ☐ dilute HCl, or washing soda
- ☐ dilute NaOH, or vinegar
- ☐ Epsom salt (magnesium sulfate)
- ☐ household ammonia cleaner
- ☐ hydrogen peroxide—6% (from hair dresser) or 3% from drugstore
- ☐ isopropyl alcohol (approx. 90%)
- ☐ liquid chlorine bleach
- ☐ liquid dish soap or detergent
- ☐ Manganese dioxide (MnO_2), sodium iodide (NaI) or potassium iodide (KI)
- ☐ Milk of Magnesia
- ☐ mossy zinc (purchase online)
- ☐ potassium nitrate fertilizer (from garden store) (cigarette ash could also be used)
- ☐ Various substances to test such as:
  - ☐ lemon, grapefruit or orange juice
  - ☐ plain yogurt
  - ☐ hydrogen peroxide
  - ☐ soil in water
  - ☐ milk
  - ☐ distilled water
  - ☐ powdered antacid

MATERIALS NEEDED FOR THE ACTIVITIES IN THIS BOOK

- [ ] liquid soap
- [ ] toothpaste
- [ ] egg white
- [ ] Milk of Magnesia
- [ ] oven cleaner
- [ ] toilet bowl cleaner
- [ ] washing soda (sodium carbonate)
- [ ] zinc sulfate (from garden store)

www.ingramcontent.com/pod-product-compliance
Lightning Source LLC
Chambersburg PA
CBHW080440170426
43195CB00017B/2836